EASY BREAD

100 No-Knead Recipes

Judith Fertig

All of the recipes in this book were previously published in *200 Fast & Easy Artisan Breads*, published in 2009 by Robert Rose Inc.

For complete cataloguing information, see page 224.

Disclaimer
The recipes in this book have been carefully tested by our kitchen and our tasters. To the best of our knowledge, they are safe and nutritious for ordinary use and users. For those people with food or other allergies, or who have special food requirements or health issues, please read the suggested contents of each recipe carefully and determine whether or not they may create a problem for you. All recipes are used at the risk of the consumer.

We cannot be responsible for any hazards, loss or damage that may occur as a result of any recipe use.

For those with special needs, allergies, requirements or health problems, in the event of any doubt, please contact your medical adviser prior to the use of any recipe.

At the time of publication, all URLs linked to existing websites. Robert Rose Inc. is not responsible for maintaining, and does not endorse the content of, any website or content not created by Robert Rose Inc.

Design: adapted from *Pain*, designed by Gabrielle Lecomte
Layout and Production: PageWave Graphics Inc.
Editor: Kathleen Fraser
Indexer: Gillian Watts
Recipe Photography: André Noël (anoelphoto.com)
Food Styling: Simon Roberge
Additional Photography: © Getty Images (front cover, back cover, linen texture, pages 3, 6, 10, 13, 14, 16, 19, 20, 23, 34, 37, 55, 77, 93, 125, 137, 151, 173, 195, 196, 199, 200, 203, 207, 209, 211, 214, 224)

Published by Robert Rose Inc.
120 Eglinton Avenue East, Suite 800, Toronto, Ontario, Canada M4P 1E2
Tel: (416) 322-6552 Fax: (416) 322-6936
www.robertrose.ca

Printed and bound in China

1 2 3 4 5 6 7 8 9 LEO 29 28 27 26 25 24 23 22 21

For my family

CONTENTS

INTRODUCTION

Although artisan bread baking is a time-honored tradition, with classic forms and methods, there has been a recent surge of revision. Baking experts, food scientists and innovative bread bloggers have taken a fresh look at old recipes and come up with new, easier ways to achieve the same or similar results.

As a cookbook author, culinary instructor and avocational baker, I've built on their expertise and gone a step further in streamlining artisan bread baking into an achievable — and rewarding — activity for busy people.

I've also used a sequential, step-by-step approach. With each dough, with each recipe, you learn and master new techniques.

The result is Easy Bread, which shows how you can achieve incredible results in just minutes a day.

Your hands-on activity (not including rising, resting or baking time) with these breads is only minutes a day. You can make the dough one day, form and bake in the days afterward.

You master easy methods for shaping the dough into round loaves (boules), baguettes, batards, rolls, filled rolls, flatbreads, pizzas, bagels, pastries and more.

You learn similarly easy, streamlined ways to make complements to bread, such as artisan butter (in the food processor in 5 minutes) and caramelized onions (in the slow cooker).

A SIMPLE METHOD FOR EVERYONE

- ▶ Use basic equipment: a large mixing bowl, a Danish dough whisk or wooden spoon, measuring cups, a cutting board or cookie sheet, an instant-read thermometer, a serrated knife, a rolling pin, a broiler pan and a baking stone.
- ▶ Make enough dough for several loaves, store the dough in the refrigerator, then bake when you're ready. Many of the doughs keep in the refrigerator for over a week.
- ▶ Skip traditional bread-making steps. No need to proof (active dry) yeast over water to make sure it works; you use instant or bread machine yeast and simply stir it into the flour. No need to knead, as you use a moist dough that does the work of activating the gluten for you. No need to bake the bread the same day — you can if you want to, but you can also wait several days, up to a week or more.
- ▶ Know when your bread is done in one easy step — by using an instant-read thermometer. No tapping, thumping, guessing, hoping.

If you can bake a batch of brownies from a box mix, you are ready to start Easy Bread. So let's get started!

Part 1
LET'S GET STARTED

LET'S GET STARTED

One-bowl, no-knead artisan bread. Is it as easy as it sounds? Let's get some hands-on experience.

If you follow the steps in making the dough, forming the loaves and baking the bread, you can't go wrong. Each easy step takes you closer to great artisan bread — and helps you avoid common pitfalls experienced by novice bread bakers.

So relax. Just follow the steps and you're on your way to your first boules and baguettes.

POINTERS FOR SUCCESS WITH ALL YOUR BREADS

- ▶ If you just scoop the flour out of the bag and dump it in the bowl, you could end up with a heavy, lackluster loaf, but by measuring the flour correctly, you'll end up with just the right amount.
- ▶ If you add hot water, it can kill the yeast and your bread won't rise, but by taking the temperature of the water, you'll know it is lukewarm.
- ▶ If you only thump or tap to test for doneness, you could end up with bread that is still gummy inside, but by taking the temperature of your loaf, you'll know it's done.

Equipment

Each piece of kitchen equipment listed below is simple but necessary to homemade artisan bread, from the start of making the dough to the process of baking it. To make the first master recipe, Easy Artisan Dough, you'll need basic kitchenware, including a wooden spoon or a Danish dough whisk. If you've never seen a dough whisk before, you'll be amazed at how often you'll use it once you get one. The dough whisk has a long wooden handle, and the whisk end looks like a freeform mitten made with thick stainless steel wire. The dough whisk does a great job with all of the doughs in this book, but is especially effective with heavier whole-grain doughs.

You'll also need something with which to slide your bread onto the baking stone in the oven. A simple three-sided cookie sheet will do, but as you get going, you might want to purchase a wooden baker's peel, sort of a flat shovel for getting breads and pizzas in the oven.

A flexible cutting board is indispensable for scooping up and sliding baguettes or batards from the floured surface to the baker's peel or baking stone. The baking stone helps replicate the even heating of a brick oven. The broiler pan of water underneath it adds steam for better baking results.

ESSENTIAL EQUIPMENT

- ▶ Measuring cups and spoons (liquid and dry)
- ▶ Instant-read thermometer
- ▶ 16-cup (4 L) mixing bowl
- ▶ Wooden spoon or Danish dough whisk
- ▶ Serrated knife
- ▶ Dough scraper
- ▶ Three-sided cookie sheet or baker's peel
- ▶ Flexible cutting board
- ▶ Baking stone
- ▶ Broiler pan

Ingredients

The basic ingredients for artisan bread are also simple, but each one is crucial to success.

YEAST

To bake artisan bread the easy way, you'll need instant or bread machine yeast, which is packaged in jars, in individual packets or in larger vacuum-sealed bags. Active dry or quick-rise yeasts need to be proofed in water first, and we're eliminating that step. The smaller granules of instant or bread machine yeast can simply be stirred into the flour and other dry ingredients. Because of the way instant or bread machine yeast is formulated, you'll use a little bit more of it than you're used to with active dry yeast bread recipes. Once you've opened your instant or bread machine yeast jar or vacuum-sealed bag, store it in the refrigerator so it stays fresh longer.

▸ **Temperature affects it.**
Both manufactured and wild yeasts in the air slow down their activity in a cold refrigerator and go into hibernation in the freezer. (That's why you can buy frozen yeast bread dough, then come home and bake it off.) Warmer temperatures help yeast release carbon dioxide to be trapped within the muscular layers of gluten, helping bread to rise. According to food scientist Shirley Corriher in *BakeWise*, manufactured yeast is most active between 86°F (30°C) and 95°F (35°C), while wild yeasts prefer lower temperatures. Yeast cells die between 138°F (59°C) and 140°F (60°C). For the artisan baker, this means that judging the temperature of liquids you stir into the dry ingredients is very important — use your instant-read thermometer so you don't inadvertently kill the yeast with hot liquids. Knowing how yeast works helps you understand the mechanics of baking better: how the bread rises in the hot oven until the dough itself reaches between 138°F (59°C) and 140°F (60°C), and then the excess moisture bakes out, the crust forms and the bread is done at 190°F (90°C).

▸ **Leaving yeast to do its work slowly results in bread with better, more developed flavor.**
So room temperature resting and rising, or even an overnight stay in the refrigerator, results in tastier bread.

FLOUR

Artisan bread made with a no-knead method requires flour with good protein content, because protein equals gluten. Gluten helps form the muscular structure of bread, thereby helping it rise. It can be activated either by kneading, which we're not going to do, or by adding extra liquid, which we are. The more gluten, the better rise we'll get in the bread. Unbleached all-purpose flour and bread flour have the protein and gluten content we're looking for. With some recipes, you can use either/or, while others specify bread flour to do really heavy lifting. If you want to use unbleached organic flours, all the better. Why unbleached flour? Because with less processing, unbleached flours retain more of their protein.

BAKING WITH CANADIAN BREAD FLOUR

Canadian bread flour generally has a higher protein content than U.S. bread flour. That means it absorbs more water. If using Canadian bread flour, you may need to use slightly more water to avoid a dry dough. Begin by adding an extra tablespoon or two (15 to 30 mL) of water and continue adding until a soft dough is formed.

SALT

We'll start off using table salt, but as we go along and get to purer artisan baking, we'll want the good stuff: fine kosher or sea salt. You can certainly use fine kosher or sea salt for all the recipes, if you wish.

WATER

We'll start off by using tap water, but as we go along, we'll use filtered or bottled spring water, as it has fewer chemicals and a purer, cleaner taste. (If you like, use filtered or bottled water for every recipe.) Use your instant-read thermometer to measure the temperature of the water in the first few recipes; eventually, you'll be able to tell by touch how warm the water needs to be. Hot water, 138°F (59°C) and above, will kill the yeast.

Ten Basic Steps to Artisan Bread

Now that we have the equipment and ingredients, what will we do with them?

1 **MEASURE.** How you measure the flour makes an enormous difference in the final product. If you just stick a measuring cup in a bag or container of flour and scoop, the flour packs into the measuring cup more. One cup (250 mL) of scooped flour will weigh around 5¼ ounces (about 157 g). If you spoon flour from the bag or container into the measuring cup, leveling it off with a knife or your finger, the flour gently settles in. One cup (250 mL) of spooned flour will weigh around 4½ ounces (about 140 g). Multiply that by the number of cups you need in a recipe, and you'll see that the measuring method makes a big difference. More flour means denser, heavier baked goods. And that's not what we want. So we'll spoon and measure.

2 **MIX.** Because we're working with instant or bread machine yeast, we'll stir the dry ingredients together first — usually the yeast, flour and salt — then stir in the liquid. We'll stir the dough together until just moistened, then beat 40 strokes, just as you would with brownie batter made from a mix. The dough should be lumpy, but it will get smoother and bigger as it rests and rises.

3 **RISE.** Now we'll let the yeast, flour and water do their work. The yeast will give off carbon dioxide bubbles, and the water will join with the gluten in the flour to form fibrous bands. The result is dough that rises. Cover the bowl with plastic wrap — it's easy to get the wrap to stick if you moisten the rim of the bowl with a little water, then attach the wrap. If you like, spray the underside of the plastic wrap, where the dough might touch, with olive oil before covering the bowl, so the dough won't stick as it rises. Let the dough rise at room temperature (72°F/22°C) for 2 hours or until it has risen nearly to the top of the bowl, or about doubled in bulk, and has a sponge-like appearance. If your kitchen is warmer, this may take less time. If your kitchen is cooler, it may take a little longer. The dough will even rise in the refrigerator.

4 **USE RIGHT AWAY OR REFRIGERATE.** Use the dough to bake that day or place the bowl of dough, covered with plastic wrap, in the refrigerator for up to 9 days before baking. Each master dough recipe has a different "use by" date; some sweetened, naturally leavened or enriched doughs will only last several days in the refrigerator. Just read the recipe to make sure. If you like, use a permanent marker to write the date you made the dough on the top of the plastic wrap.

5 FORM. To form loaves, rolls, flatbreads and more, you'll remove half or one-quarter of the dough with a serrated knife and a dough scraper — or you might use all of it. The serrated knife helps mark the line on top and through the dough; the dough scraper helps remove the dough from the bowl. Each recipe will give you a guideline as to how big the portion should be: the size of a softball for a quarter of the dough, or the size of a small volleyball for half the dough. It doesn't matter if your dough portion isn't exact; the bread will be happy and delicious anyway, and you'll be using an instant-read thermometer to tell when it is done, so don't worry. After you've taken some of the dough out of the bowl, the remaining dough will deflate somewhat, but it will rise again.

You'll transfer your portion of dough to a floured surface and dust it very lightly with flour. You'll also want to flour your hands, because no-knead doughs are fibrous and stickier than doughs you knead. Work the dough as little as possible and sprinkle on flour as necessary. You want enough flour that you'll be able to work the dough, with the help of your dough scraper, without it sticking to your hands, but not so much flour that you'll get a heavy loaf. When the dough is soft but not sticky, you've added enough flour.

Next, you'll form the dough into a geometric shape, depending on the type of bread you're making: circle, oval, rectangle, cylinder and so on. This dough won't form precise shapes, so don't worry about getting it just right. The main thing is to form the loaf so that the surface has a soft, non-sticky skin, without any cracks or seams. Pinch any seams together to prevent "blow-outs" as the loaf bakes. Lightly flour any sticky places on the dough. The dough should feel soft and smooth all over, like a baby's skin, but not at all sticky.

6 REST. Sprinkle cornmeal on a three-sided cookie sheet or baker's peel and place the dough on the cornmeal. Cover with a tea towel and let rest at room temperature for 40 minutes.

7 PREPARE OVEN FOR ARTISAN BAKING. About 30 minutes before baking, place a broiler pan on the lower shelf and a baking stone on the middle shelf of the oven. Preheat the oven to 450°F (230°C). Most of the artisan breads in this book need the high temperature to do their final rise in the hot oven.

8 SLASH WITH SERRATED KNIFE. When it's ready to bake, the dough won't have risen much, but it will finish rising dramatically in the oven. For many (but not all) of the breads, you'll use a serrated knife to make evenly spaced diagonal slashes, about ½ to 1 inch (1 to 2.5 cm) deep, across the loaf, exposing the moist dough under the surface. The slashes help the bread bake more evenly and add an attractive pattern where the exposed moist dough "blows out."

Every bowl of master dough will make at least two to four different breadstuffs, from boules and baguettes to batards, breadsticks, flatbreads, pizzas, rolls, bagels, coffee cakes, pastries and more.

9 **SLIDE FORMED DOUGH ONTO BAKING STONE AND ADD WATER TO BROILER PAN.** First, make sure the dough isn't sticking to the cookie sheet by scooping under it in several places with the dough scraper. The cornmeal will act as little ball bearings to help move the dough from the cookie sheet to the hot baking stone. If you like, practice this beforehand. Using a quick forward-and-back jerk of your arms, slide the dough from the cornmeal-dusted cookie sheet back onto the floured surface, so you feel more confident. You'll see that it's a lot easier than it seems. When you're ready, use an oven mitt to carefully pull the middle rack of the oven out several inches. Hold the cookie sheet level with the rack, so that the dough will slide onto the center of the hot baking stone. With a quick forward jerk of your arms, slide the formed dough from the cookie sheet to the stone. If your baguette, for example, doesn't land straight on the baking stone, use a long-handled metal pancake turner to push it into shape (but even an irregular baguette will be delicious). Push the middle rack back in place. Pull the lower rack out, pour hot water into the broiler pan and push the lower rack back in place. Close the oven door immediately so the steam will envelop the oven. When we get to the intermediate and advanced recipes, you'll be spraying the dough with water before and during baking to help create a blistered crust. And as we go along, you'll be able to slide two loaves onto the baking stone.

10 **BAKE.** Keep the oven light on in the beginning so you can see how the bread bakes. At first, the formed dough won't appear to do anything. A couple of minutes in, it will start to rise dramatically and the slashed seams will burst open (but hopefully not any "hidden" seams you didn't pinch closed; even if this happens, though, your irregular bread will be delicious).

You don't have to wonder if your bread is done, because you'll test it with an instant-read thermometer inserted in the center of the loaf. When the thermometer registers at least 190°F (90°C), your bread is done. As you bake more, you'll know by how fast the needle goes around or the temperature jumps that your bread is done. No thumping, tapping, worrying. You'll know. Wearing oven mitts, remove the loaves by hand to cool on a wire rack.

Characteristics of Easy Artisan Dough

If you've baked kneaded breads before, this dough will seem looser to you — and it is! The extra moisture in the dough takes the place of kneading in activating the gluten in the flour. Gluten helps to form those muscular bands that are the structure of bread, trapping the carbon dioxide released by the yeast. When you work with the dough, use as little flour as possible and use the dough scraper as much as possible to scrape up the dough from the floured surface, turn it and even cut it. Use a pastry brush to brush away excess flour. The dough will feel more like a baby's skin than the tight doughs you usually get with a kneading method.

The looser dough also means that these breads are looser in shape. You won't get tight spirals, intricate braids, close knots or other exact forms. The Cardamom and Cinnamon–Scented Swedish Tea Ring (page 139), for example, will have a rustic, feathery appearance instead of the neat and tidy loaf you see in the grocery store.

Each master dough recipe will tell you what type of color, crust and crumb to expect from the finished product. Along the way, you'll learn how to achieve all the various types.

THE 3 CS OF ARTISAN BREAD

- **Color:** In artisan bread, color comes from the interplay of flour and heat. Depending on the type of flour you use, your dough may be creamy white, pale yellow, beige, reddish brown, flecked brown or dark brown. Flavorings such as puréed squash, beer and saffron, as well as herbs, fruits, seeds and spices that you stir or fold into the dough, also contribute to color and appearance.
- **Crumb:** The texture of the bread's interior. Each master dough recipe will produce a slightly different type of crumb, from the moist and soft custard crumb of Easy Artisan Dough to the rich and buttery crumb of Easy Artisan Brioche Dough.
- **Crust:** The top exterior of the bread. Your bread crusts will also vary with each master dough: a crisp crust with Easy Artisan Dough; a shiny, buttery crust with Easy Artisan Brioche Dough; and a crisp and shiny crust with Easy Artisan Bagel Dough.

Easy Artisan Dough

Makes enough dough for bread, rolls, pizza or flatbread to serve 12 to 16

This first master recipe introduces you to the basics of this easy artisan bread method. As you begin to make bread, all of this will get even easier. You won't have to check the temperature of the water, as you'll know what lukewarm feels like. You'll get quite good at forming the various types of loaves and sliding them onto the hot baking stone. You'll be able to tell, by how fast the temperature rises on the instant-read thermometer, when your bread reaches 190°F (90°C) and is done. Your artisan loaves will have a crisp, darkened crust, a tender, moist crumb and a mellow, toasty flavor — all with this easy method. The dough will also make delicious rolls, pizza or flatbread.

INGREDIENTS

6½ cups (1.625 L) unbleached all-purpose or bread flour

1½ tbsp (22 mL) instant or bread machine yeast

1½ tbsp (22 mL) fine table or kosher salt

3 cups (750 mL) lukewarm water (about 100°F/38°C)

EQUIPMENT

Instant-read thermometer

16-cup (4 L) mixing bowl

Wooden spoon or Danish dough whisk

METHOD

1 Spoon the flour into a measuring cup, level with a knife or your finger, then dump the flour into the mixing bowl.

2 Add the yeast and salt to the flour. Stir together with a wooden spoon or Danish dough whisk. Pour in the water and stir together until just moistened. Beat 40 strokes, scraping the bottom and the sides of the bowl, until the dough forms a lumpy, sticky mass.

3 Cover the bowl with plastic wrap and let rise at room temperature (72°F/22°C) in a draft-free place for 2 hours or until the dough has risen nearly to the top of the bowl and has a sponge-like appearance.

4 Use that day or place the dough, covered with plastic wrap, in the refrigerator for up to 9 days before baking.

TIPS

- Combining 1½ cups (375 mL) hot with 1½ cups (375 mL) cold tap water will result in lukewarm water of approximately 100°F (38°C).
- Before storing the dough in the refrigerator, use a permanent marker to write the date on the plastic wrap, so you'll know when you made your dough — and when to use it up 9 days later.

BAKING WITH CANADIAN BREAD FLOUR

Canadian bread flour generally has a higher protein content than U.S. bread flour. That means it absorbs more water. If using Canadian bread flour, you may need to use slightly more water to avoid a dry dough. Begin by adding an extra tablespoon or two (15 to 30 mL) of water and continue adding until a soft dough is formed.

Baguette

Makes 1 baguette, to serve 4

A crusty baguette — warm from the oven — can be a regular feature of your weeknight repertoire when you have the dough ready-made in the refrigerator. Form the baguette and let the dough relax while you prepare the rest of dinner, then pop the baguette in the oven to bake.

INGREDIENTS

$\frac{1}{4}$ recipe prepared Easy Artisan Dough (page 22), about the size of a softball

Unbleached all-purpose or bread flour

$\frac{1}{4}$ cup (50 mL) cornmeal

2 cups (500 mL) hot water

EQUIPMENT

Three-sided cookie sheet, flexible cutting board or baker's peel

Broiler pan

Baking stone

METHOD

1 Place dough on a floured surface and dust very lightly with flour. Flour your hands. Working the dough as little as possible and adding flour as necessary, form the dough into a 14-inch (35 cm) cylinder. Smooth the dough with your hands to form a soft, non-sticky skin. Pinch any seams together. Pinch each end into a point. Lightly flour any sticky places on the dough. The dough should feel soft and smooth all over, but not at all sticky.

2 Sprinkle the cornmeal on the cookie sheet and place the dough cylinder on the cornmeal. Cover with a tea towel and let rest at room temperature for 40 minutes.

3 About 30 minutes before baking, place the broiler pan on the lower shelf and the baking stone on the middle shelf of the oven. Preheat to 450°F (230°C).

4 Using a serrated knife, make three evenly spaced diagonal slashes, about $\frac{1}{2}$ inch (1 cm) deep, across the baguette, exposing the moist dough under the surface.

5 Carefully pull the middle rack of the oven out several inches. Hold the cookie sheet level with the rack so that the baguette will slide sideways onto the center of the hot stone. With a quick forward jerk of your arms, slide the baguette from the board to the stone. Push the middle rack back in place. Pull the lower rack out, pour the hot water into the broiler pan and push the lower rack back in place. Close the oven door immediately so the steam will envelop the oven.

6 Bake for 25 minutes or until the crust is a medium dark brown and an instant-read thermometer inserted in the center of the loaf registers at least 190°F (90°C). Remove the loaf to cool on a wire rack.

TIP

When you are proficient at sliding the dough onto the baking stone, you can bake two baguettes at one time. Place the baguettes on the prepared cookie sheet so that they are parallel to each other and about 6 inches (15 cm) apart. Then hold the cookie sheet level with the rack so that the first baguette will slide sideways onto the hot baking stone. With a quick forward jerk of your arms, slide the first baguette from the cookie sheet to the back of the stone. With another jerk, slide the second baguette onto the front of the stone.

Baby Boule

Makes 1 round loaf, or boule, to serve 4

This recipe makes a small boule, which will rise dramatically in the oven, producing a crusty loaf with a moist and tender crumb, which four people can greedily consume. Delicious! And so easy!

INGREDIENTS

$\frac{1}{4}$ recipe prepared Easy Artisan Dough (page 22), about the size of a softball

Unbleached all-purpose or bread flour

$\frac{1}{4}$ cup (50 mL) cornmeal

2 cups (500 mL) hot water

EQUIPMENT

Three-sided cookie sheet, flexible cutting board or baker's peel

Broiler pan

Baking stone

METHOD

1 Place dough on a floured surface and dust very lightly with flour. Flour your hands. Working the dough as little as possible and adding flour as necessary, form the dough into a 6-inch (15 cm) round. Smooth the dough with your hands to form a soft, non-sticky skin. Pinch any seams together. Lightly flour any sticky places on the dough. The dough should feel soft and smooth all over, but not at all sticky.

2 Sprinkle the cornmeal on the cookie sheet and place the dough round on the cornmeal. Cover with a tea towel and let rest at room temperature for 40 minutes.

3 About 30 minutes before baking, place the broiler pan on the lower shelf and the baking stone on the middle shelf of the oven. Preheat to 450°F (230°C).

4 Using a serrated knife, make three evenly spaced slashes, about $\frac{1}{2}$ inch (1 cm) deep, across the boule, exposing the moist dough under the surface.

5 Carefully pull the middle rack of the oven out several inches. Hold the cookie sheet level with the rack so that the dough round will slide onto the center of the hot stone. With a quick forward jerk of your arms, slide the dough round from the cookie sheet to the stone. Push the middle rack back in place. Pull the lower rack out, pour the hot water into the broiler pan and push the lower rack back in place. Close the oven door immediately so the steam will envelop the oven.

6 Bake for 27 to 30 minutes or until the crust is a medium dark brown and an instant-read thermometer inserted in the center of the loaf registers at least 190°F (90°C). Remove the loaf to cool on a wire rack.

TIP

When you are proficient at sliding the dough onto the baking stone, you can bake two boules at one time, if it's big enough to allow enough space between them. Place the boules on the prepared cookie sheet so that they are parallel to each other and about 4 inches (10 cm) apart. Then hold the cookie sheet level with the rack so that the boules will slide onto the hot baking stone. With a quick forward jerk of your arms, slide the boules from the cookie sheet to each side of the stone.

Batard

Makes 1 large loaf, to serve 8 to 10

Use half of the dough to form a larger loaf, to be baked without a loaf pan. This bread has a dark crust, a mellow flavor and a soft crumb.

INGREDIENTS

$\frac{1}{2}$ recipe prepared Easy Artisan Dough (page 22), about the size of a volleyball

Unbleached all-purpose or bread flour

$\frac{1}{2}$ cup (125 mL) cornmeal

2 cups (500 mL) hot water

EQUIPMENT

Three-sided cookie sheet

Flexible cutting board, floured, or two metal spatulas

Broiler pan

Baking stone

METHOD

1 Place dough on a floured surface and dust very lightly with flour. Flour your hands. Working the dough as little as possible and adding flour as necessary, form the dough into a 14-inch (35 cm) cylinder. Pinch the ends and any seams closed. Lightly flour any sticky places on the dough. The dough should feel soft and smooth all over, but not at all sticky.

2 Sprinkle the cornmeal on the cookie sheet. Using the cutting board or two metal spatulas, transfer the loaf to the prepared cookie sheet. Cover with a tea towel and let rest at room temperature for 40 minutes.

3 About 30 minutes before baking, place the broiler pan on the lower shelf and the baking stone on the middle shelf of the oven. Preheat to 450°F (230°C).

4 Using a serrated knife, make five cross-hatch slashes, about $\frac{1}{2}$ inch (1 cm) deep, diagonally across the top of the loaf, exposing the moist dough under the surface.

5 Carefully pull the middle rack of the oven out several inches. Hold the cookie sheet level with the rack so that the loaf will slide sideways onto the hot stone. With a quick forward jerk of your arms, slide the loaf from the cookie sheet to the stone. If necessary, use a metal spatula to reposition the loaf. Push the middle rack back in place. Pull the lower rack out, pour the hot water into the broiler pan and push the lower rack back in place. Close the oven door immediately so the steam will envelop the oven.

6 Bake for 25 to 27 minutes or until the crust is dark brown and an instant-read thermometer inserted in the center of the loaf registers at least 190°F (90°C). Remove the loaf to cool on a wire rack.

Rolls

Makes 4 rolls

You can also make crusty artisan rolls with the master dough. They will look small before baking, but will at least double in size in the hot oven. They do not get as dark as the boule, baguette or loaf. These rolls are big enough to use for sandwiches — for burgers, grilled chicken or the filling of your choice.

INGREDIENTS

$\frac{1}{4}$ recipe prepared Easy Artisan Dough (page 22), about the size of a softball

Unbleached all-purpose or bread flour

$\frac{1}{4}$ cup (50 mL) cornmeal

2 cups (500 mL) hot water

EQUIPMENT

Three-sided cookie sheet, flexible cutting board or baker's peel

Broiler pan

Baking stone

METHOD

1 Place dough on a floured surface and dust very lightly with flour. Flour your hands. Working the dough as little as possible and adding flour as necessary, form the dough into an 8-inch (20 cm) cylinder. With a dough scraper, slice the cylinder into 2-inch (5 cm) pieces. Pinch the cut ends together. Lightly flour any sticky places on the dough. The dough should feel soft and smooth all over, but not at all sticky.

2 Sprinkle the cornmeal on the cookie sheet. Arrange the rolls in two horizontal lines, 4 inches (10 cm) apart, on the prepared cookie sheet. Cover with a tea towel and let rest at room temperature for 40 minutes.

3 About 30 minutes before baking, place the broiler pan on the lower shelf and the baking stone on the middle shelf of the oven. Preheat to 450°F (230°C).

4 Slash rolls with serrated knife. Using a serrated knife, make two cross-hatch slashes, about $\frac{1}{2}$ inch (1 cm) deep, in the top center of each roll, exposing the moist dough under the surface.

5 Slide rolls onto baking stone and add water to broiler pan. Carefully pull the middle rack of the oven out several inches. Hold the cookie sheet level with the rack so that the rolls will slide sideways onto the hot stone. With a quick forward jerk of your arms, slide the rolls from the cookie sheet to the stone. If a roll lands too close to another, use a metal spatula to reposition it. Push the middle rack back in place. Pull the lower rack out, pour the hot water into the broiler pan and push the lower rack back in place. Close the oven door immediately so the steam will envelop the oven.

6 Bake for 15 to 17 minutes or until the crust is lightly browned and an instant-read thermometer inserted in the center of a roll registers at least 190°F (90°C). Remove rolls to cool on a wire rack.

Pizza Blanca

Makes 1 pizza, to serve 4

This artisan-style pizza features simple toppings — olive oil, garlic and cheese — but can be customized with the toppings of your choice.

INGREDIENTS

$\frac{1}{4}$ recipe prepared Easy Artisan Dough (page 22), about the size of a softball

Unbleached all-purpose or bread flour

2 tbsp (25 mL) olive oil

1 clove garlic, minced

$\frac{1}{2}$ cup (125 mL) grated Asiago, Parmesan or Romano cheese

2 cups (500 mL) hot water

EQUIPMENT

Rolling pin

12-inch (30 cm) round perforated pizza pan

Broiler pan

Baking stone

METHOD

1 Place dough on a floured surface and dust very lightly with flour. Flour your hands and the rolling pin. Working the dough as little as possible and adding flour as necessary, roll out the dough into a 12-inch (30 cm) circle. Lightly flour any sticky places on the dough as you roll. The dough should feel gently taut and smooth all over, but not at all sticky.

2 Drape the dough over the rolling pin and transfer to the prepared pan. Pat into place. Cover with a tea towel and let rest at room temperature for 40 minutes.

3 About 30 minutes before baking, place the broiler pan on the lower shelf and the baking stone on the middle shelf of the oven. Preheat to 450°F (230°C).

4 In a small, bowl, combine olive oil and garlic. Brush onto the dough and sprinkle with cheese.

5 Place the pizza pan on the hot stone. Pull the lower rack out, pour the hot water into the broiler pan, and push the lower rack back in place. Close the oven door immediately so the steam will envelop the oven.

6 Bake for 15 minutes or until the edges of the crust and the cheese have both browned.

TIP

This type of thin-crust pizza is not meant for heavy sauce, cheese and meat toppings. Instead, use toppings that add bold flavor without bulk, such as thinly sliced onion, prosciutto or crisp-cooked pancetta, grated aged cheeses, chèvre, feta or blue cheese crumbles, olives, pesto, roasted red pepper, cooked Italian sausage crumbles, thinly sliced mushrooms, fresh herbs, fresh tomatoes, oil-packed sun-dried tomatoes, thin asparagus stalks or arugula.

Part 2
NOW YOU'RE BAKING

NOW YOU'RE BAKING

Once you know how to make Easy Artisan Dough, form the basic bread shapes and bake with the artisan method, it's time to add a little more to your repertoire.

True to the easy method of making artisan bread, we'll take easy artisan steps. With each master dough recipe, you'll learn a little more method, technique and science, and by the end of the book, you'll feel confident making Danish pastries, flaky croissants and homemade bagels.

In this part, we'll start by adding a few more basic bread shapes, like Baby Baguettes (page 40), a boat-shaped batard (page 52) and pizza (page 74). You'll learn how to roll out the dough, spread on a filling and roll it up to form swirled loaves and rolls. Then we'll go on to include whole grains in a variety of ways: as dry packaged flour, freshly ground flour and even cooked cereal, in breads such as Oatmeal Honey Bread (page 70). After that, it's how to incorporate a filling into the dough or coat it with seeds for even more variety, as in Peshawari Naan (page 90). Then we're on to flavoring the dough itself, with buttermilk, beer, spices, purées, herbs and more, as in Mini Hamburger Buns (page 106).

By the time we're on to slow-rise breads such as Slow-Rise Ciabatta (page 122), which require a yeast starter and an overnight rest, you'll be quite the accomplished artisan baker. You'll be ready for something sweet — maybe Classic Cinnamon Rolls (page 142), or coffee cake, or Apple Custard Kuchen (page 146) — made with a sweetened, egg-enriched dough. Not to mention all the glazes and fillings that go with these goodies. Once you've got that type of dough mastered, you'll be ready for Butternut Brioche Dough (page 152) and Cider-Glazed Savarin (page 162), the epitome of a sweetened, egg-enriched dough and the glory of French bakers.

Easy Artisan Dough

Makes enough dough for bread, rolls, pizza or flatbread to serve 12 to 16

Now let's put this dough through its paces — in more varied forms. With a bowl of this dough in your refrigerator, warm and crusty breads are about an hour away.

INGREDIENTS

6½ cups (1.625 L) unbleached all-purpose or bread flour

1½ tbsp (22 mL) instant or bread machine yeast

1½ tbsp (22 mL) fine table or kosher salt

3 cups (750 mL) lukewarm water (about 100°F/38°C)

EQUIPMENT

Instant-read thermometer

16-cup (4 L) mixing bowl

Wooden spoon or Danish dough whisk

METHOD

1 Spoon the flour into a measuring cup, level with a knife or your finger, then dump the flour into the mixing bowl.

2 Add the yeast and salt to the flour. Stir together with a wooden spoon or Danish dough whisk. Pour in the water and stir together until just moistened. Beat 40 strokes, scraping the bottom and the sides of the bowl, until the dough forms a lumpy, sticky mass.

3 Cover the bowl with plastic wrap and let rise at room temperature (72°F/22°C) in a draft-free place for 2 hours or until the dough has risen nearly to the top of the bowl and has a sponge-like appearance.

4 Use that day or place the dough, covered with plastic wrap, in the refrigerator for up to 9 days before baking.

TIP

Combining 1½ cups (375 mL) hot with 1½ cups (375 mL) cold tap water will result in lukewarm water of approximately 100°F (38°C).

BAKING WITH CANADIAN BREAD FLOUR

Canadian bread flour generally has a higher protein content than U.S. bread flour. That means it absorbs more water. If using Canadian bread flour, you may need to use slightly more water to avoid a dry dough. Begin by adding an extra tablespoon or two (15 to 30 mL) of water and continue adding until a soft dough is formed.

EASY ARTISAN BREADS IN MINUTES A DAY

Day 1: Stir the dough together and let rise. Bake, or cover and chill.

Days 2–9: Remove part of the dough, form and bake.

Boule

Makes 1 large round loaf, or boule, to serve 8

Once you've made the Baby Boule in Part 1, it's easy to go a step further and make it twice as big. This time, you'll remove half the dough from the bowl and form it into a round loaf.

INGREDIENTS

½ recipe prepared Easy Artisan Dough (page 36), about the size of a volleyball

Unbleached all-purpose or bread flour

½ cup (125 mL) cornmeal

2 cups (500 mL) hot water

EQUIPMENT

Three-sided cookie sheet, flexible cutting board or baker's peel

Broiler pan

Baking stone

METHOD

1 Place dough portion on a floured surface and dust very lightly with flour. Flour your hands. Working the dough as little as possible and adding flour as necessary, form the dough into a 12-inch (30 cm) round. Smooth the dough with your hands to form a soft, non-sticky skin. Pinch any seams together. Lightly flour any sticky places on the dough. The dough should feel soft and smooth all over, but not at all sticky.

2 Sprinkle the cornmeal on the cookie sheet and place the dough round on the cornmeal. Cover with a tea towel and let rest at room temperature for 40 minutes.

3 About 30 minutes before baking, place the broiler pan on the lower shelf and the baking stone on the middle shelf of the oven. Preheat to 450°F (230°C).

4 Using a serrated knife, make three evenly spaced slashes, about ½ inch (1 cm) deep, across the boule, exposing the moist dough under the surface.

5 Carefully pull the middle rack of the oven out several inches. Hold the cookie sheet level with the rack so that the dough round will slide onto the center of the hot stone. With a quick forward jerk of your arms, slide the dough round from the cookie sheet to the stone. Push the middle rack back in place. Pull the lower rack out, pour the hot water into the broiler pan and push the lower rack back in place. Close the oven door immediately so the steam will envelop the oven.

6 Bake for 27 to 30 minutes or until the crust is a medium dark brown and an instant-read thermometer inserted in the center of the loaf registers at least 190°F (90°C). Remove the loaf to cool on a wire rack.

VARIATION

Add texture and variety to your artisan bread by using 3 cups (750 mL) whole-grain flour (white whole wheat, semolina or whole wheat) plus 3½ cups (875 mL) unbleached all-purpose or unbleached bread flour to equal the 6½ cups (1.625 L) in the master recipe.

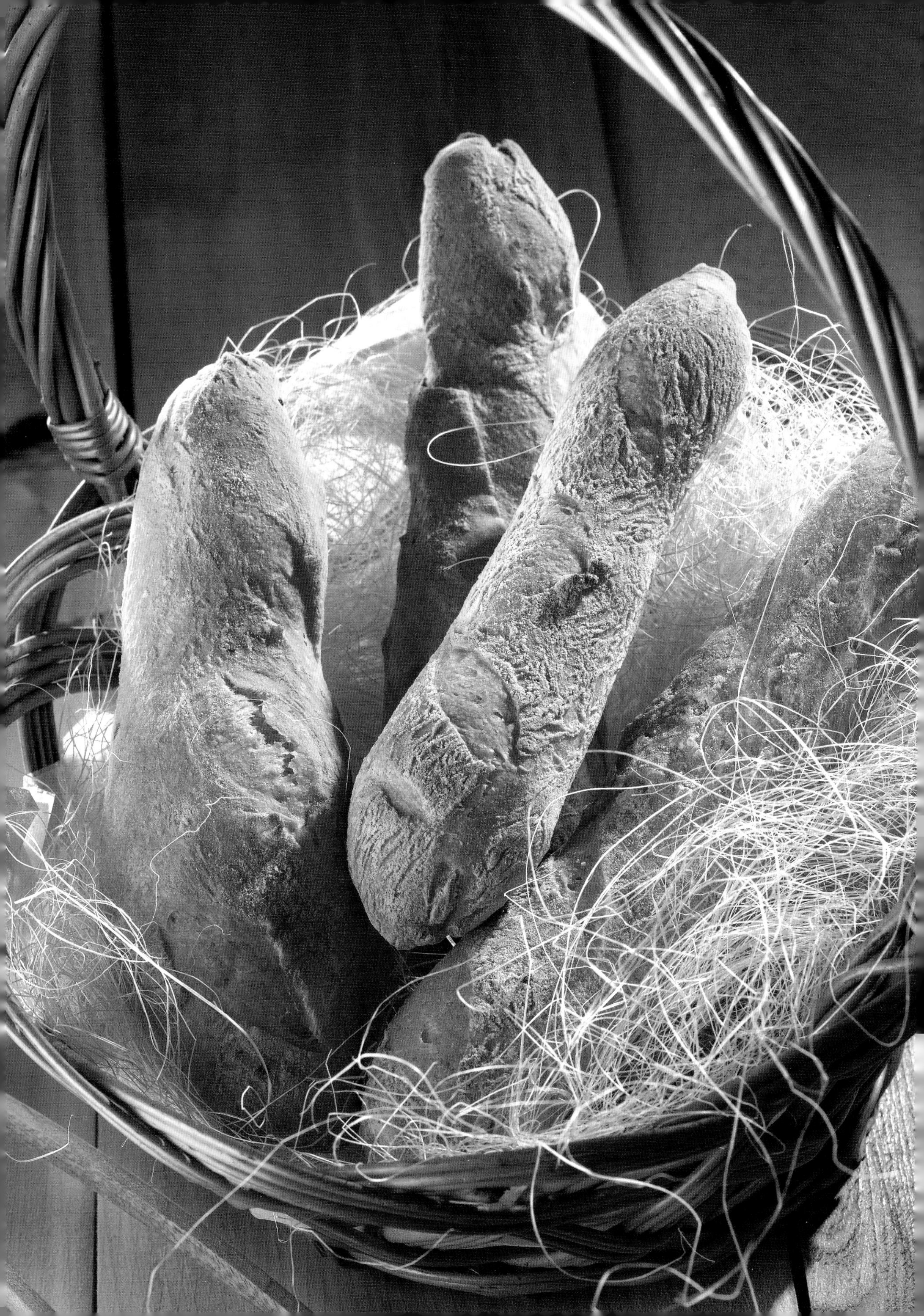

Baby Baguettes

Makes 4 baby baguettes

If you can form a larger baguette, you can make smaller ones. This recipe makes four baby baguettes for individual servings. Form the baguettes and let the dough rest while you prepare dinner, then pop the baguettes in the oven to bake.

INGREDIENTS

1/4 recipe prepared Easy Artisan Dough (page 36), about the size of a softball

Unbleached all-purpose or bread flour

1/4 cup (50 mL) cornmeal

2 cups (500 mL) hot water

EQUIPMENT

Three-sided cookie sheet, flexible cutting board or baker's peel

Broiler pan

Baking stone

METHOD

1 Place dough on a floured surface and dust very lightly with flour. Flour your hands. Working the dough as little as possible and adding flour as necessary, form the dough into a 12-inch (30 cm) cylinder. With a dough scraper, cut the dough into four 3-inch (7.5 cm) segments. Shape each segment into a baguette. Smooth the dough with your hands to form a soft, non-sticky skin. Pinch any seams together. Pinch each end into a point. Lightly flour any sticky places on the dough. The dough should feel soft and smooth all over, but not at all sticky.

2 Sprinkle the cornmeal on the cookie sheet and place the baguettes in two rows on the cornmeal. Cover with a tea towel and let rest at room temperature for 40 minutes.

3 About 30 minutes before baking, place the broiler pan on the lower shelf and the baking stone on the middle shelf of the oven. Preheat to 450°F (230°C).

4 Slash baguettes with serrated knife. Using a serrated knife, make three evenly spaced diagonal slashes, about 1/2 inch (1 cm) deep, across each baguette, exposing the moist dough under the surface.

5 Carefully pull the middle rack of the oven out several inches. Hold the cookie sheet level with the rack so that the first row of baguettes will slide sideways onto the center of the hot stone. With a quick forward jerk of your arms, slide the baguettes from the cookie sheet to the back of the stone. Then with the same motion, slide the second row of baguettes onto the front of the stone. Push the middle rack back in place. Pull the lower rack out, pour the hot water into the broiler pan and push the lower rack back in place. Close the oven door immediately so the steam will envelop the oven.

6 Bake for 12 to 15 minutes or until the crust is a medium dark brown and an instant-read thermometer inserted in the center of a baguette registers at least 190°F (90°C). Remove baguettes to cool on a wire rack.

TIP

If you have a leftover baguette, let it cool, place in a large plastic freezer bag (or cut the baguette in half and place 2 halves in a bag) and freeze for up to 3 months. To warm a frozen baguette, wrap it in foil and place in a 350°F (230°C) oven for 15 to 20 minutes or until warmed through.

Naan

Makes 8 flatbreads

Brushed with melted butter or ghee before baking, puffy ovals of naan are meant to help scoop up the flavorful curries of northern India. Try these easy ones first, before going on to Traditional Naan (page 71) made with all-purpose and whole wheat flours or Peshawari Naan (page 90), with dried fruit, herbs and nuts incorporated into the dough.

INGREDIENTS

$\frac{1}{4}$ recipe prepared Easy Artisan Dough (page 36), about the size of a softball

Unbleached all-purpose or bread flour

$\frac{1}{4}$ cup (50 mL) cornmeal

Melted butter or olive oil

2 cups (500 mL) hot water

EQUIPMENT

Rolling pin

Large baking sheet

Broiler pan

Baking stone

Metal spatula

METHOD

1 Place dough on a floured surface and dust very lightly with flour. Flour your hands and the rolling pin. Working the dough as little as possible and adding flour as necessary, form the dough into an 8-inch (20 cm) cylinder. With a dough scraper, cut the dough into 1-inch (2.5 cm) slices. Roll out each slice into a 6-inch (15 cm) long oval. Lightly flour any sticky places on the dough. The dough should feel soft and smooth all over, but not at all sticky.

2 Sprinkle the cornmeal on the cookie sheet and place the dough ovals on the cornmeal. Cover with a tea towel and let rest at room temperature for 40 minutes.

3 About 30 minutes before baking, place the broiler pan on the lower shelf and the baking stone on the middle shelf of the oven. Preheat to 450°F (230°C).

4 Brush the naan with melted butter.

5 Carefully pull the middle rack of the oven out several inches. With a metal spatula, place four naan on the hot stone. Pull the lower rack out, pour the hot water into the broiler pan and push the lower rack back in place. Close the oven door immediately so the steam will envelop the oven.

6 Bake for 7 to 8 minutes or until the crust is lightly blistered. Remove the naan to cool on a wire rack. Repeat the baking process with the remaining naan.

Pita Bread

Makes 4 flatbreads

Pita bread — which rises higher than naan — is meant to scoop up hummus or other Middle Eastern spreads, or to be split in half to hold sandwich fillings.

INGREDIENTS

$\frac{1}{4}$ recipe prepared Easy Artisan Dough (page 36), about the size of a softball

Unbleached all-purpose flour

$\frac{1}{4}$ cup (50 mL) cornmeal

Melted butter or olive oil

2 cups (500 mL) hot water

EQUIPMENT

Rolling pin

Baking sheet

Broiler pan

Baking stone

Metal spatula

METHOD

1 Place dough on a floured surface and dust very lightly with flour. Flour your hands and the rolling pin. Working the dough as little as possible and adding flour as necessary, form the dough into an 8-inch (20 cm) cylinder. With a dough scraper, cut the dough into 2-inch (5 cm) slices. Roll out each slice into a 6-inch (15 cm) round. Lightly flour any sticky places on the dough. The dough should feel soft and smooth all over, but not at all sticky.

2 Sprinkle the cornmeal on the cookie sheet and place the dough rounds on the cornmeal. Cover with a tea towel and let rest at room temperature for 40 minutes.

3 About 30 minutes before baking, place the broiler pan on the lower shelf and the baking stone on the middle shelf of the oven. Preheat to 450°F (230°C).

4 Brush the pitas with melted butter.

5 Carefully pull the middle rack of the oven out several inches. With a metal spatula, place pitas on the hot stone. Pull the lower rack out, pour the hot water into the broiler pan and push the lower rack back in place. Close the oven door immediately so the steam will envelop the oven.

6 Bake for 6 to 8 minutes or until puffed and light brown. Remove the pitas to cool on a wire rack.

Soft Pretzels

Makes 8 soft pretzels

Once you've made breadsticks, you're ready for pretzels. What gives pretzels their distinctive flavor is lye — a dry, caustic substance also known as caustic soda or sodium hydroxide. You can find it in the plumbing aisle of hardware stores. You need only a very little, mixed into boiling water, in which to dip each formed pretzel before baking. You can omit the lye wash, but your pretzels will taste like breadsticks.

INGREDIENTS

$\frac{1}{4}$ recipe prepared Easy Artisan Dough (page 34), about the size of a softball

Unbleached all-purpose flour

$\frac{1}{2}$ cup (125 mL) cornmeal

1 cup (250 mL) boiling water

1 tsp (5 mL) lye

Coarse kosher salt or pretzel salt

2 cups (500 mL) hot water

EQUIPMENT

4-cup (1 L) heatproof glass measuring cup or bowl

Three-sided cookie sheet, flexible cutting board or baker's peel

Tongs

Broiler pan

Baking stone

METHOD

1 Place dough on a floured surface and dust very lightly with flour. Flour your hands. Working the dough as little as possible and adding flour as necessary, pat the dough into an 8-inch (20 cm) square. Lightly flour any sticky places on the dough. The dough should feel soft and smooth all over, but not at all sticky.

2 Using a pizza wheel or a sharp knife, cut the square into eight 1-inch (2.5 cm) wide strips. Gently pull and squeeze each strip to lengthen it to 14 inches (35 cm). Holding an end of a strip in each hand, cross one hand over the other to form a pretzel shape. Press the ends into the body of the pretzel.

3 Cover with a tea towel and let rest at room temperature for 40 minutes.

4 About 30 minutes before baking, place the broiler pan on the lower shelf and the baking stone on the middle shelf of the oven. Preheat to 450°F (230°C).

5 Right before baking, combine the boiling water and lye in the heatproof measuring cup. Sprinkle the cornmeal on the cookie sheet. Using tongs, dip each pretzel in the hot lye mixture, let drain briefly and place about 2 inches (5 cm) apart on the cornmeal. Pour the remaining lye mixture down the drain and wash out the bowl. Sprinkle the pretzels with salt.

6 Carefully pull the middle rack of the oven out several inches. Hold the cookie sheet level with the rack so that the pretzels will slide onto the hot stone. With a quick forward jerk of your arms, slide the pretzels from the cookie sheet to the stone. If a pretzel lands too close to another, use a metal spatula to reposition it. Push the middle rack back in place. Pull the lower rack out, pour the hot water into the broiler pan and push the lower rack back in place. Close the oven door immediately so the steam will envelop the oven.

7 Bake for 17 to 19 minutes or until well browned. Remove the pretzels to cool on a wire rack.

VARIATION

You can also use Easy Artisan Whole-Grain Dough (page 54), made with semolina, or Caraway Rye Dough (page 58).

Cheddar Pretzels

Dust each pretzel with 1 tbsp (15 mL) powdered Cheddar cheese (available in bulk and online) before sprinkling with salt.

Fougasse

Makes 1 flatbread, to serve 4 to 6

What's focaccia to Italians is fougasse to the French — an artisan flatbread, usually with a savory flavor. The trick with fougasse is to create the diagonal slits that, when opened, make the distinctive leafy pattern in the bread.

INGREDIENTS

$\frac{1}{4}$ recipe prepared Easy Artisan Dough (page 36), about the size of a softball

Unbleached all-purpose flour

1 tbsp (15 mL) olive oil

2 cups (500 mL) hot water

EQUIPMENT

Rolling pin

Large baking sheet, lined with parchment paper

Broiler pan

Baking stone

METHOD

1 Place dough on a floured surface and dust very lightly with flour. Flour your hands and the rolling pin. Working the dough as little as possible and adding flour as necessary, roll out the dough into a 12- by 6-inch (30 by 15 cm) oval. Lightly flour any sticky places on the dough. The dough should feel soft and smooth all over, but not at all sticky.

2 Using a pizza wheel or a sharp knife, cut two rows of four diagonal slashes evenly spaced along the length of the oval, about 2 to 3 inches (5 to 7.5 cm) long, that almost meet in the middle of the dough, like this: /\. Transfer the dough to the prepared baking sheet and pull the top and sides of the dough to stretch it into a larger oval with opened slits. Brush the surface of the dough with the olive oil.

3 Cover with a tea towel and let rest at room temperature for 40 minutes.

4 About 30 minutes before baking, place the broiler pan on the lower shelf and the baking stone on the middle shelf of the oven. Preheat to 450°F (230°C).

5 Carefully pull the middle rack of the oven out several inches. Place the baking sheet on the hot stone. Push the middle rack back in place. Pull the lower rack out, pour the hot water into the broiler pan and push the lower rack back in place. Close the oven door immediately so the steam will envelop the oven.

6 Bake for 17 to 20 minutes or until the crust is medium brown. Transfer to a wire rack to cool.

Flatbread with Caramelized Onions and Brie

Makes 1 flatbread, to serve 4 as an entrée or 8 as an appetizer

As an entrée for a casual meal or cut into squares for an appetizer, this flatbread always gets rave reviews.

INGREDIENTS

¼ recipe prepared Easy Artisan Dough (page 34), about the size of a softball

Unbleached all-purpose flour

1 cup (250 mL) Easy Caramelized Onions (page 196)

8 oz (250 g) Brie cheese (rind on), cut into 1-inch (2.5 cm) pieces

2 cups (500 mL) hot water

EQUIPMENT

8-inch (20 cm) square metal baking pan, greased

Broiler pan

Baking stone

METHOD

1 Place dough on a floured surface and dust very lightly with flour. Flour your hands. Working the dough as little as possible and adding flour as necessary, pat the dough into an 8-inch (20 cm) square. Lightly flour any sticky places on the dough. The dough should feel soft and smooth all over, but not at all sticky.

2 Transfer the dough to the prepared pan and pat to fit. Using the handle of a wooden spoon, dimple the flatbread at 2-inch (5 cm) intervals.

3 Using a fork, spread the caramelized onions over the top of the flatbread, then dot with Brie.

4 Cover with a tea towel and let rest at room temperature for 40 minutes.

5 About 30 minutes before baking, place the broiler pan on the lower shelf and the baking stone on the middle shelf of the oven. Preheat to 450°F (230°C).

6 Carefully pull the middle rack of the oven out several inches. Place the pan of flatbread on the hot stone. Push the middle rack back in place. Pull the lower rack out, pour the hot water into the broiler pan and push the lower rack back in place. Close the oven door immediately so the steam will envelop the oven.

7 Bake for 25 to 27 minutes or until the crust is lightly browned. Remove from pan and transfer to a wire rack to cool.

Heirloom Tomato Flatbread

After patting the flatbread into the pan, dimple the dough, then top with 8 fresh basil leaves. Arrange 1 cup (250 mL) chopped fresh heirloom tomatoes (try golden or orange heirlooms) on top of the basil. Sprinkle with ½ cup (125 mL) freshly grated Parmesan cheese and drizzle with 2 tbsp (25 mL) olive oil.

Caprese Swirl Rolls

Makes 12 rolls

These easy savory swirled rolls are delicious as cocktail, tailgate or casual meal fare. This version is a take on the traditional Caprese salad of fresh tomatoes, basil and mozzarella.

INGREDIENTS

½ recipe prepared Easy Artisan Dough (page 36), about the size of a volleyball

Unbleached all-purpose flour

½ cup (125 mL) pesto

1 cup (250 mL) finely chopped tomatoes

1 cup (250 mL) finely chopped fresh mozzarella cheese (bocconcini)

2 cups (500 mL) hot water

EQUIPMENT

Rolling pin

Baking sheet, lined with parchment paper

Broiler pan

Baking stone

METHOD

1 Place dough on a floured surface and dust very lightly with flour. Flour your hands and the rolling pin. Working the dough as little as possible and adding flour as necessary, roll out the dough into a 16- by 10-inch (40 by 25 cm) rectangle. Spread pesto over the dough, leaving a ½-inch (1 cm) perimeter. Scatter tomatoes and mozzarella over the pesto. Starting with a long end, roll up the dough into a cylinder. If the dough begins to stick to the surface, use a dough scraper to push flour under the dough and scrape it up. Gently press and squeeze as you're rolling, to form the dough into a solid cylinder. The cylinder will lengthen to 18 inches (45 cm). With a pastry brush, brush off any excess flour. Pinch the ends and long seam closed, then turn seam side down. With the dough scraper, slice the cylinder into twelve 1½-inch (4 cm) pieces.

2 Place the rolls, cut side up, about 2 inches (5 cm) apart on the prepared baking sheet. Cover with a tea towel and let rest at room temperature for 40 minutes.

3 About 30 minutes before baking, place the broiler pan on the lower shelf and the baking stone on the middle shelf of the oven. Preheat to 450°F (230°C).

4 Carefully pull the middle rack of the oven out several inches. Place the baking sheet on the hot stone. Push the middle rack back in place. Pull the lower rack out, pour the hot water into the broiler pan and push the lower rack back in place. Close the oven door immediately so the steam will envelop the oven.

5 Bake for 13 to 15 minutes or until the rolls are risen and browned. Transfer to a wire rack to cool on baking sheet.

VARIATION

You can also use Easy Artisan Whole-Grain Dough (page 54), made with semolina.

Caramelized Onion and Brie Rolls

Substitute 1 cup (250 mL) Easy Caramelized Onions (page 196) and 1 cup (250 mL) finely chopped Brie cheese (with the rind on) for the pesto, tomatoes and mozzarella.

Sicilian Swirl Rolls

Substitute 1/2 cup (125 mL) prepared pizza sauce for the pesto and 1 cup (250 mL) crumbled cooked Italian sausage for the tomatoes.

Greek-Style Pizza

Makes 1 pizza, to serve 4

All the flavors of a good Greek salad can also be had in this crisp-crusted pizza.

INGREDIENTS

1/4 recipe prepared Easy Artisan Dough (page 36), about the size of a softball

Unbleached all-purpose flour

1 cup (250 mL) chopped tomatoes

1/2 cup (125 mL) sliced pitted kalamata olives

1/2 cup (125 mL) crumbled feta cheese

2 tbsp (25 mL) olive oil

2 cups (500 mL) hot water

1 cup (250 mL) packed baby arugula

EQUIPMENT

Rolling pin

12-inch (30 cm) round perforated pizza pan

Broiler pan

Baking stone

METHOD

1 Place dough on a floured surface and dust very lightly with flour. Flour your hands and the rolling pin. Working the dough as little as possible and adding flour as necessary, roll out the dough into a 12-inch (30 cm) round. Lightly flour any sticky places on the dough as you roll. The dough should feel gently taut and smooth all over, but not at all sticky.

2 Drape the dough over the rolling pin and transfer to the pizza pan. Pat into place. Cover with a tea towel and let rest at room temperature for 40 minutes.

3 About 30 minutes before baking, place the broiler pan on the lower shelf and the baking stone on the middle shelf of the oven. Preheat to 450°F (230°C).

4 Sprinkle tomatoes, olives and feta over the dough, then drizzle with olive oil.

5 Place the pizza pan on the hot stone. Pull the lower rack out, pour the hot water into the broiler pan and push the lower rack back in place. Close the oven door immediately so the steam will envelop the oven.

6 Bake for 15 minutes or until the edges of the crust have browned. Place the arugula in the center of the pizza. To serve, cut the pizza into wedges.

TIP

When you are proficient at sliding dough onto the baking stone, you can place the unbaked pizza on a cornmeal-sprinkled baker's peel instead of using the pizza pan. With a quick forward jerk of your arms, slide the pizza from the baker's peel onto the stone.

VARIATION

Try Easy Artisan Whole-Grain Dough (page 54), made with semolina or white whole wheat flour.

Pizza Margherita

Prepare through Step 3. Top the dough with 3 plum (Roma) tomatoes, cut lengthwise into $\frac{1}{2}$-inch (1 cm) slices, 8 fresh basil leaves, cut into shreds, and 8 oz (250 g) fresh mozzarella cheese (bocconcini), cut into $\frac{1}{2}$-inch (1 cm) slices. Drizzle with 2 tbsp (25 mL) olive oil. Bake for 15 to 17 minutes or until lightly browned.

Pizza Funghi

Prepare through Step 3. Top the dough with 8 oz (250 g) thinly sliced portobello or cremini mushrooms, 2 tbsp (25 mL) chopped fresh flat-leaf (Italian) parsley and $\frac{1}{2}$ cup (125 mL) freshly grated Parmesan cheese. Drizzle with 2 tbsp (25 mL) olive oil. Bake for 15 to 17 minutes or until lightly browned.

Easy Artisan Whole-Grain Dough

Makes enough dough for bread, rolls, pizza or flatbread to serve 12 to 16

Adding whole-grain flours to artisan dough increases the flavor, texture and fiber in the bread. These flours can be finely or more coarsely ground, whichever you prefer. It's easy to substitute 2 cups (500 mL) of a gluten-rich whole-grain flour (see page 55) for 2 cups (500 mL) unbleached all-purpose or bread flour in the Easy Artisan Dough recipe, as here. If you wish to use low-gluten or no-gluten flour (see page 55) for the whole-grain component, counter it by using unbleached bread flour instead of all-purpose for the regular flour component, as unbleached bread flour has more protein to make gluten (and make up for the lack of it in low-gluten flours).

INGREDIENTS

$4\frac{1}{2}$ cups (1.125 L) unbleached all-purpose or bread flour

2 cups (500 mL) gluten-rich whole-grain flour (see page 55)

2 tbsp (25 mL) instant or bread machine yeast

$1\frac{1}{2}$ tbsp (22 mL) fine table or kosher salt

3 cups (750 mL) lukewarm water (about 100°F/38°C)

EQUIPMENT

Instant-read thermometer

16-cup (4 L) mixing bowl

Wooden spoon or Danish dough whisk

METHOD

1 One at a time, spoon the unbleached flour and whole-grain flour into a measuring cup, level with a knife or your finger, then dump into the mixing bowl. Combine well.

2 Add the yeast and salt to the flours. Stir together with a wooden spoon or Danish dough whisk. Pour in the water and stir together until just moistened. Beat 40 strokes, scraping the bottom and the sides of the bowl, until the dough forms a lumpy, sticky mass.

3 Cover the bowl with plastic wrap and let rise at room temperature (72°F/22°C) in a draft-free place for 2 hours or until the dough has risen nearly to the top of the bowl and has a sponge-like appearance.

4 Use that day or place the dough, covered with plastic wrap, in the refrigerator for up to 3 days before baking.

TIPS

- To increase the amount of protein in unbleached all-purpose flour when using it with low-gluten or no-gluten flour, add 1 tsp (2 mL) Artisan Bread Dough Enhancer (page 194) to each cup (250 mL) all-purpose flour.
- Combining $1\frac{1}{2}$ cups (375 mL) hot with $1\frac{1}{2}$ cups (375 mL) cold tap water will result in lukewarm water of approximately 100°F (38°C).
- Before storing the dough in the refrigerator, use a permanent marker to write the date on the plastic wrap, so you'll know when you made your dough — and when to use it up 3 days later.

HIGH-GLUTEN WHOLE-GRAIN FLOURS

Atta (Indian whole wheat flour for roti, naan and chapati)
Whole wheat flour
White whole wheat flour
Graham flour (coarsely ground whole wheat)
Semolina or durum wheat flour
Sprouted whole-grain hard winter wheat flour

NO-GLUTEN OR LOW-GLUTEN WHOLE-GRAIN FLOURS

Amaranth flour
Chickpea (garbanzo bean) flour
Corn flour
Millet flour
Oat flour
Quinoa flour
Rice flour (glutinous or brown)
Rye flour
Soy flour
Spelt flour
Tapioca flour
Teff flour

BAKING WITH CANADIAN BREAD FLOUR

Canadian bread flour generally has a higher protein content than U.S. bread flour. That means it absorbs more water. If using Canadian bread flour, you may need to use slightly more water to avoid a dry dough. Begin by adding an extra tablespoon or two (15 to 30 mL) of water and continue adding until a soft dough is formed.

EASY ARTISAN BREADS IN MINUTES A DAY

Day 1: Stir the dough together and let rise. Bake, or cover and chill.
Days 2–9: Remove part of the dough, form and bake.

Cracked Wheat Dough

Makes enough dough for bread, rolls, pizza or flatbread to serve 12 to 16

Put your hot winter breakfast cereal to good use in this dough.

INGREDIENTS

1½ cups (375 mL) uncooked cracked wheat cereal

½ cup (125 mL) liquid honey

1½ tbsp (22 mL) unsalted butter

1½ tsp (7 mL) salt

1⅔ cups (400 mL) boiling water

4½ cups (1.125 L) unbleached all-purpose or bread flour

2 tbsp (25 mL) instant or bread machine yeast

1½ tbsp (22 mL) fine table or kosher salt

3 cups (750 mL) lukewarm water (about 100°F/38°C)

EQUIPMENT

Instant-read thermometer

16-cup (4 L) mixing bowl

Wooden spoon or Danish dough whisk

METHOD

1 In a bowl, combine wheat cereal, honey, butter and salt. Pour in boiling water, stir and let stand for 15 minutes or until the cereal has softened and the mixture is still warm (100°F/38°C), but not hot.

2 Spoon the flour into a measuring cup, level with a knife or your finger, then dump the flour into the mixing bowl.

3 Add the wheat cereal mixture, yeast and salt to the flour. Stir together with a wooden spoon or Danish dough whisk. Pour in the water and stir together until just moistened. Beat 40 strokes, scraping the bottom and the sides of the bowl, until the dough forms a lumpy, sticky mass.

4 Cover the bowl with plastic wrap and let rise at room temperature (72°F/22°C) in a draft-free place for 2 hours or until the dough has risen nearly to the top of the bowl and has a sponge-like appearance.

5 Use that day or place the dough, covered with plastic wrap, in the refrigerator for up to 3 days before baking.

Daily Grind Whole Wheat Dough

Makes enough dough for bread, rolls, pizza or flatbread to serve 12 to 16

The nutty flavor of freshly ground wheat comes through in this dough.

INGREDIENTS

$4\frac{1}{2}$ cups (1.125 L) unbleached all-purpose or bread flour

2 cups (500 mL) freshly ground whole wheat kernels

2 tbsp (25 mL) instant or bread machine yeast

$1\frac{1}{2}$ tbsp (22 mL) fine table or kosher salt

3 cups (750 mL) lukewarm water (about 100°F/38°C)

EQUIPMENT

Instant-read thermometer

16-cup (4 L) mixing bowl

Wooden spoon or Danish dough whisk

METHOD

1 One at a time, spoon the flour and ground whole wheat kernels into a measuring cup, level with a knife or your finger, then dump into the mixing bowl. Combine well.

2 Add the yeast and salt to the flour mixture. Stir together with a wooden spoon or Danish dough whisk. Pour in the water and stir together until just moistened. Beat 40 strokes, scraping the bottom and the sides of the bowl, until the dough forms a lumpy, sticky mass.

3 Cover the bowl with plastic wrap and let rise at room temperature (72°F/22°C) in a draft-free place for 2 hours or until the dough has risen nearly to the top of the bowl and has a sponge-like appearance.

4 Use that day or place the dough, covered with plastic wrap, in the refrigerator for up to 3 days before baking.

TIP

Three cups (750 mL) whole wheat kernels will grind into about 7 cups (1.75 L) fine whole wheat flour.

BAKING WITH CANADIAN BREAD FLOUR

Canadian bread flour generally has a higher protein content than U.S. bread flour. That means it absorbs more water. If using Canadian bread flour, you may need to use slightly more water to avoid a dry dough. Begin by adding an extra tablespoon or two (15 to 30 mL) of water and continue adding until a soft dough is formed.

Caraway Rye Dough

Makes enough dough for bread, rolls, pizza or flatbread to serve 12 to 16

The classic combination of caraway seeds, rye flour and molasses makes a darker, more flavorful dough.

INGREDIENTS

4½ cups (1.125 L) unbleached bread flour

2 cups (500 mL) rye flour

2 tbsp (25 mL) instant or bread machine yeast

2 tbsp (25 mL) caraway seeds

1½ tbsp (22 mL) fine table or kosher salt

⅓ cup (75 mL) light (fancy) molasses

3 cups (750 mL) lukewarm water (about 100°F/38°C)

EQUIPMENT

Instant-read thermometer

16-cup (4 L) mixing bowl

Wooden spoon or Danish dough whisk

METHOD

1 One at a time, spoon the bread flour and rye flour into a measuring cup, level with a knife or your finger, then dump into the mixing bowl. Combine well.

2 Add the yeast, caraway seeds and salt to the flours. Stir together with a wooden spoon or Danish dough whisk. Stir molasses into the water. Pour into the flour mixture and stir together until just moistened. Beat 40 strokes, scraping the bottom and the sides of the bowl, until the dough forms a lumpy, sticky mass.

3 Cover the bowl with plastic wrap and let rise at room temperature (72°F/22°C) in a draft-free place for 2 hours or until the dough has risen nearly to the top of the bowl and has a sponge-like appearance.

4 Use that day or place the dough, covered with plastic wrap, in the refrigerator for up to 3 days before baking.

Oatmeal Honey Dough

Makes enough dough for bread, rolls, pizza or flatbread to serve 12 to 16

Mellow and slightly sweet, bread made from this dough is great toasted.

INGREDIENTS

4½ cups (1.125 L) unbleached bread flour

2 cups (500 mL) large-flake (old-fashioned) rolled oats

2 tbsp (25 mL) instant or bread machine yeast

1½ tbsp (22 mL) fine table or kosher salt

⅓ cup (75 mL) wildflower, clover or other pale amber liquid honey

3 cups (750 mL) lukewarm water (about 100°F/38°C)

EQUIPMENT

Instant-read thermometer

16-cup (4 L) mixing bowl

Wooden spoon or Danish dough whisk

METHOD

1 One at a time, spoon the flour and oats into a measuring cup, level with a knife or your finger, then dump into the mixing bowl. Combine well.

2 Add the yeast and salt to the flour mixture. Stir together with a wooden spoon or Danish dough whisk. Stir honey into the water. Pour into the flour mixture and stir together until just moistened. Beat 40 strokes, scraping the bottom and the sides of the bowl, until the dough forms a lumpy, sticky mass.

3 Cover the bowl with plastic wrap and let rise at room temperature (72°F/22°C) in a draft-free place for 2 hours or until the dough has risen nearly to the top of the bowl and has a sponge-like appearance.

4 Use that day or place the dough, covered with plastic wrap, in the refrigerator for up to 3 days before baking.

BAKING WITH CANADIAN BREAD FLOUR

Canadian bread flour generally has a higher protein content than U.S. bread flour. That means it absorbs more water. If using Canadian bread flour, you may need to use slightly more water to avoid a dry dough. Begin by adding an extra tablespoon or two (15 to 30 mL) of water and continue adding until a soft dough is formed.

Traditional Naan Dough

Makes enough dough for flatbread to serve 12 to 16

Traditional naan dough is made with a combination of maida (fine all-purpose flour) and atta (whole wheat flour). Look for maida and atta at Indian grocers.

INGREDIENTS

4½ cups (1.125 L) unbleached all-purpose flour

2 cups (500 mL) atta (Indian whole wheat flour)

2 tbsp (25 mL) instant or bread machine yeast

1½ tbsp (22 mL) fine table or kosher salt

1 cup (250 mL) plain yogurt

3 cups (750 mL) lukewarm water (about 100°F/38°C)

EQUIPMENT

Instant-read thermometer

16-cup (4 L) mixing bowl

Wooden spoon or Danish dough whisk

METHOD

1 One at a time, spoon the all-purpose flour and atta into a measuring cup, level with a knife or your finger, then dump into the mixing bowl. Combine well.

2 Add the yeast and salt to the flours. Stir together with a wooden spoon or Danish dough whisk. Stir yogurt into the water. Pour into the flour mixture and stir together until just moistened. Beat 40 strokes, scraping the bottom and the sides of the bowl, until the dough forms a lumpy, sticky mass.

3 Cover the bowl with plastic wrap and let rise at room temperature (72°F/22°C) in a draft-free place for 2 hours or until the dough has risen nearly to the top of the bowl and has a sponge-like appearance.

4 Use that day or place the dough, covered with plastic wrap, in the refrigerator for up to 3 days before baking.

Provençal Socca Dough

Makes enough dough for flatbread to serve 12 to 16

The nutty flavor of chickpeas (garbanzo beans) comes through in this dough from the south of France.

INGREDIENTS

4½ cups (1.125 L) unbleached bread flour

2 cups (500 mL) chickpea (garbanzo bean) flour

2 tbsp (25 mL) instant or bread machine yeast

1½ tbsp (22 mL) fine table or kosher salt

3 cups (750 mL) lukewarm water (about 100°F/38°C)

EQUIPMENT

Instant-read thermometer

16-cup (4 L) mixing bowl

Wooden spoon or Danish dough whisk

BAKING WITH CANADIAN BREAD FLOUR

Canadian bread flour generally has a higher protein content than U.S. bread flour. That means it absorbs more water. If using Canadian bread flour, you may need to use slightly more water to avoid a dry dough. Begin by adding an extra tablespoon or two (15 to 30 mL) of water and continue adding until a soft dough is formed.

METHOD

1 One at a time, spoon the bread flour and chickpea flour into a measuring cup, level with a knife or your finger, then dump into the mixing bowl. Combine well.

2 Add the yeast and salt to the flours. Stir together with a wooden spoon or Danish dough whisk. Pour in the water and stir together until just moistened. Beat 40 strokes, scraping the bottom and the sides of the bowl, until the dough forms a lumpy, sticky mass.

3 Cover the bowl with plastic wrap and let rise at room temperature (72°F/22°C) in a draft-free place for 2 hours or until the dough has risen nearly to the top of the bowl and has a sponge-like appearance.

4 Use that day or place the dough, covered with plastic wrap, in the refrigerator for up to 3 days before baking.

Cracked Wheat Baguettes

Makes 2 baguettes, to serve 8

These baguettes have just a little more texture and heightened flavor from the cooked cracked wheat cereal added to the dough. In this recipe, you'll be sliding two baguettes onto the baking stone.

INGREDIENTS

½ recipe prepared Cracked Wheat Dough (page 56), about the size of a volleyball

Unbleached all-purpose or bread flour

½ cup (125 mL) cornmeal

2 cups (500 mL) hot water

EQUIPMENT

Three-sided cookie sheet, flexible cutting board or baker's peel

Broiler pan

Baking stone

METHOD

1 Place dough on a floured surface and dust very lightly with flour. Flour your hands. Form the dough into a 12-inch (30 cm) log. Using a dough scraper, cut the dough into two equal portions. Working the dough as little as possible and adding flour as necessary, form each dough portion into a 14-inch (35 cm) cylinder. Smooth the dough with your hands to form a soft, non-sticky skin. Pinch any seams together. Pinch each end into a point. Lightly flour any sticky places on the dough. The dough should feel soft and smooth all over, but not at all sticky.

2 Sprinkle the cornmeal on the cookie sheet and place the baguettes on the cornmeal so that they are parallel to each other and about 6 inches (15 cm) apart. Cover with a tea towel and let rest at room temperature for 40 minutes.

3 About 30 minutes before baking, place the broiler pan on the lower shelf and the baking stone on the middle shelf of the oven. Preheat to 450°F (230°C).

4 Using a serrated knife, make three evenly spaced diagonal slashes, about 1 inch (2.5 cm) deep, across each baguette, exposing the moist dough under the surface.

5 Carefully pull the middle rack of the oven out several inches. Hold the cookie sheet level with the rack so that the first baguette will slide sideways onto the hot stone. With a quick forward jerk of your arms, slide the first baguette from the cookie sheet to the back of the stone. With another jerk, slide the second baguette onto the front of the stone. Make sure they're at least 4 inches (10 cm) apart. Push the middle rack back in place. Pull the lower rack out, pour the hot water into the broiler pan and push the lower rack back in place. Close the oven door immediately so the steam will envelop the oven.

6 Bake for 25 to 27 minutes or until the crust is a medium dark brown and an instant-read thermometer inserted in the center of the loaves registers at least 190°F (90°C). Remove the loaves to cool on a wire rack.

TIP

If you have a leftover baguette, let it cool, place in a large plastic freezer bag (or cut the baguette in half and place 2 halves in a bag) and freeze for up to 3 months. To warm a frozen baguette, wrap it in foil and place in a 350°F (180°C) oven for 15 to 20 minutes or until warmed through.

Rustic French Boule

Makes 1 large round loaf, or boule, to serve 8

This recipe makes a large boule with enhanced flavor and texture. It will rise dramatically in the oven, producing a crusty loaf with a moist and tender crumb, which eight people can greedily consume. If you're new to whole-grain baking, start off with dough made with white whole wheat flour or semolina for the whole-grain component, as this will be more similar in flavor and texture to white bread — but a lot more interesting!

INGREDIENTS

½ recipe prepared Easy Artisan Whole-Grain Dough (page 54), about the size of a volleyball, made with white whole wheat flour or semolina

Unbleached all-purpose or bread flour

½ cup (125 mL) cornmeal

2 cups (500 mL) hot water

EQUIPMENT

Three-sided cookie sheet, flexible cutting board or baker's peel

Broiler pan

Baking stone

Plastic spray bottle of water

METHOD

1 Place dough on a floured surface and dust very lightly with flour. Flour your hands. Working the dough as little as possible and adding flour as necessary, form the dough into a 12-inch (30 cm) round. Smooth the dough with your hands to form a soft, non-sticky skin. Pinch any seams together. Lightly flour any sticky places on the dough. The dough should feel soft and smooth all over, but not at all sticky.

2 Sprinkle the cornmeal on the cookie sheet and place the dough round on the cornmeal. Cover with a tea towel and let rest at room temperature for 40 minutes.

3 About 30 minutes before baking, place the broiler pan on the lower shelf and the baking stone on the middle shelf of the oven. Preheat to 450°F (230°C).

4 Using a serrated knife, make three evenly spaced slashes, about 1 inch (2.5 cm) deep, across the boule, exposing the moist dough under the surface.

5 Carefully pull the middle rack of the oven out several inches. Hold the cookie sheet level with the rack so that the dough round will slide onto the center of the hot stone. With a quick forward jerk of your arms, slide the dough round from the cookie sheet to the stone. Push the middle rack back in place. Pull the lower rack out, pour the hot water into the broiler pan and push the lower rack back in place. Spray the boule with water. Close the oven door immediately so the steam will envelop the oven.

6 Bake for 15 minutes, then quickly open the oven door and spray the loaf with water again. Continue baking for 12 to 15 minutes or until the crust is a medium dark brown and an instant-read thermometer inserted in the center of the loaf registers at least 190°F (90°C). Remove the loaf to cool on a wire rack.

TIPS

- Note that the slashes you'll make in this denser dough are twice as deep: 1 inch (2.5 cm). Spraying the boule with water during baking will promote a crispier crust.
- White whole wheat flour is milled from hard white spring wheat with a milder flavor and lighter color than hard red winter wheat. You can use it as you would traditional whole wheat flour. If you can't find it, use regular whole wheat flour.

Amish Pinwheel Bread

Makes 1 large loaf, to serve 8 to 10

Adapted from an Amish bread recipe from northern Ohio, this two-color bread looks as good as it tastes, with an interior swirl of contrasting cream and tan. To get this effect, you can use two whole-grain doughs of different colors or pair the softer Easy Artisan Dough with Easy Artisan Whole-Grain Dough, as here.

INGREDIENTS

$\frac{1}{4}$ recipe prepared Easy Artisan Dough (page 36), about the size of a softball

$\frac{1}{4}$ recipe prepared Easy Artisan Whole-Grain Dough (page 54), about the size of a softball, made with a darker flour

Unbleached all-purpose or bread flour

$\frac{1}{2}$ cup (125 mL) cornmeal

2 cups (500 mL) hot water

EQUIPMENT

Rolling pin (optional)

Three-sided cookie sheet, flexible cutting board or baker's peel

Baking stone

Broiler pan

METHOD

1 Place dough portions on a floured surface and dust very lightly with flour. Flour your hands. Working the dough as little as possible and adding flour as necessary, roll out or pat each dough portion into a 10- by 9-inch (25 by 23 cm) rectangle. Stack one rectangle on top of the other. Starting with a long end, roll up the dough into a cylinder. If the dough begins to stick to the surface, use a dough scraper to push flour under the dough and scrape it up. Gently press and squeeze as you're rolling to form the dough into a solid cylinder. With a pastry brush, brush off any excess flour. Pinch the ends and long seam closed. Lightly flour any sticky places on the dough. The dough should feel soft and smooth all over, but not at all sticky.

2 Sprinkle the cornmeal on the cookie sheet and place the dough, seam side down, on the cornmeal. Cover with a tea towel and let rest at room temperature for 40 minutes.

3 About 30 minutes before baking, place the broiler pan on the lower shelf and the baking stone on the middle shelf of the oven. Preheat to 450°F (230°C).

4 Using a serrated knife, make five evenly spaced diagonal slashes, about 1 inch (2 cm) deep, across the loaf, exposing the moist dough under the surface.

5 Carefully pull the middle rack of the oven out several inches. Hold the cookie sheet level with the rack so that the loaf will slide sideways onto the center of the hot stone. With a quick forward jerk of your arms, slide the loaf from the cookie sheet to the stone. Push the middle rack back in place. Pull the lower rack out, pour the hot water into the broiler pan and push the lower rack back in place. Close the oven door immediately so the steam will envelop the oven.

6 Bake for 27 to 29 minutes or until the crust is a medium dark brown and an instant-read thermometer inserted in the center of the loaf registers at least 190°F (90°C). Remove the loaf to cool on a wire rack.

VARIATION

You can also use Easy Artisan Dough (page 36) paired with Caraway Rye (page 58) for contrast.

Caraway Rye Tart with Ham and Gruyère

Makes 1 tart, to serve 6 to 8

This savory tart, perfect for a casual meal, is a cross between a deep-dish pizza and a quiche. A slice of it goes well with a frosty mug of beer and a green salad. Make this tart more Alsatian with ham and Gruyère, or more Italian with sausage and Asiago.

INGREDIENTS

¼ recipe prepared Caraway Rye Dough (page 58), about the size of a softball

Unbleached bread flour

2 eggs, beaten

1 cup (250 mL) heavy or whipping (35%) cream

8 oz (250 g) ham, diced, or Italian sausage, cooked and crumbled

½ cup (125 mL) finely chopped green onions

½ cup (125 mL) shredded Gruyère or Asiago cheese

2 cups (500 mL) hot water

EQUIPMENT

Rolling pin

8-inch (20 cm) round baking pan

Broiler pan

Baking stone

METHOD

1 Place dough on a floured surface and dust very lightly with flour. Flour your hands and the rolling pin. Working the dough as little as possible and adding flour as necessary, roll out the dough into a 10-inch (25 cm) circle. Lightly flour any sticky places on the dough as you roll. The dough should feel gently taut and smooth all over, but not at all sticky.

2 Drape the dough over the rolling pin and transfer to the baking pan. Fit the dough into the bottom and up the sides of the pan. Cover with a tea towel and let rest at room temperature for 40 minutes.

3 About 30 minutes before baking, place the broiler pan on the lower shelf and the baking stone on the middle shelf of the oven. Preheat to 450°F (230°C).

4 Five minutes before baking, whisk together eggs and cream in a small bowl. Scatter ham and green onions over the tart crust and pour in the egg mixture. Sprinkle with Gruyère.

5 Carefully pull the middle rack of the oven out several inches. Place the baking pan on the hot stone. Push the middle rack back in place. Pull the lower rack out, pour the hot water into the broiler pan and push the lower rack back in place. Close the oven door immediately so the steam will envelop the oven.

6 Bake for 17 to 20 minutes or until the filling has browned and the crust has turned a medium reddish-brown. Transfer to a wire rack to cool.

Oatmeal Honey Bread

Makes 2 loaves, to serve 16

I prefer this bread baked in a pan so it's easy to slice and toast in the morning.

INGREDIENTS

1 recipe prepared Oatmeal Honey Dough (page 59)

Unbleached bread flour

2 cups (500 mL) hot water

EQUIPMENT

Two 9- by 5-inch (23 by 12.5 cm) loaf pans, greased

Broiler pan

Baking stone

METHOD

1 Place dough on a floured surface and dust very lightly with flour. Divide it in half with a serrated knife and dough scraper. Flour your hands. Working the dough as little as possible and adding flour as necessary, form each portion into an 8-inch (20 cm) cylinder. Smooth the dough with your hands to form a soft, non-sticky skin. Pinch any seams together. Lightly flour any sticky places on the dough. The dough should feel soft and smooth all over, but not at all sticky.

2 Place each cylinder in a prepared loaf pan. Cover with tea towels and let rest at room temperature for 40 minutes.

3 About 30 minutes before baking, place the broiler pan on the lower shelf and the baking stone on the middle shelf of the oven. Preheat to 400°F (200°C).

4 Carefully pull the middle rack of the oven out several inches. Place the loaf pans at least 3 inches (7.5 cm) apart on the hot stone. Push the middle rack back in place. Pull the lower rack out, pour the hot water into the broiler pan and push the lower rack back in place. Close the oven door immediately so the steam will envelop the oven.

5 Bake for 27 to 30 minutes or until the crust is a medium dark brown and an instant-read thermometer inserted in the center of the loafs registers at least 190°F (90°C). Transfer to a wire rack to cool in pans for 10 minutes. Remove from pans and let cool on rack.

Traditional Naan

Makes 8 flatbreads

Traditional naan, the flatbread of northern India, Pakistan and Afghanistan, is usually baked on the walls of a charcoal- or wood-burning tandoor oven. A tandoor is dome-shaped and made of a hard-fired terracotta — a material much like your baking stone! Traditional naan doughs are made of a combination of maida (unbleached all-purpose flour) and atta (a whole wheat flour). A little plain yogurt is mixed into the dough for moisture. To be very authentic, brush these flatbreads with ghee or melted butter before baking, but they also taste delicious brushed with olive oil.

INGREDIENTS

¼ recipe prepared Traditional Naan Dough (page 60), about the size of a softball

Unbleached all-purpose flour

¼ cup (50 mL) cornmeal

Melted butter or olive oil

2 cups (500 mL) hot water

EQUIPMENT

Rolling pin

Large baking sheet

Broiler pan

Baking stone

Metal spatula

METHOD

1 Place dough on a floured surface and dust very lightly with flour. Flour your hands and the rolling pin. Working the dough as little as possible and adding flour as necessary, form the dough into an 8-inch (20 cm) cylinder. With a dough scraper, cut the dough into 1-inch (2.5 cm) slices. Roll out each slice into a 6-inch (15 cm) long oval. Lightly flour any sticky places on the dough. The dough should feel soft and smooth all over, but not at all sticky.

2 Sprinkle the cornmeal on the baking sheet and place the dough ovals on the cornmeal. Cover with a tea towel and let rest at room temperature for 40 minutes.

3 About 30 minutes before baking, place the broiler pan on the lower shelf and the baking stone on the middle shelf of the oven. Preheat to 450°F (230°C).

4 Brush the naan with melted butter.

5 Carefully pull the middle rack of the oven out several inches. With a metal spatula, place four naan on the hot stone. Push the middle rack back in place. Pull the lower rack out, pour the hot water into the broiler pan and push the lower rack back in place. Close the oven door immediately so the steam will envelop the oven.

6 Bake for 7 to 8 minutes or until the crust is lightly blistered. Remove the naan to cool on a wire rack. Repeat the baking process with the remaining naan.

TIP

Look for maida, atta, ghee and other naan ingredients at Indian grocers.

Provençal Socca with Roasted Shallots and Garlic

Makes 1 flatbread, to serve 8 as an appetizer

Traditional Provençal socca is a thin crêpe made from chickpea (garbanzo bean) flour — a street food specialty of Van Gogh's town of Arles. This artisan version is just the thing to serve with a glass of wine for a sophisticated appetizer. Chickpea flour is available in the specialty flour section of well-stocked grocery stores.

INGREDIENTS

¼ recipe prepared Provençal Socca Dough (page 61), about the size of a softball

Unbleached bread flour

¼ cup (50 mL) cornmeal

2 cups (500 mL) Caramelized Shallots and Garlic with Red Wine (page 197)

1 tbsp (15 mL) fresh rosemary leaves

2 cups (500 mL) hot water

EQUIPMENT

Rolling pin

Baking sheet

Broiler pan

Baking stone

METHOD

1 Place dough on a floured surface and dust very lightly with flour. Flour your hands and the rolling pin. Working the dough as little as possible and adding flour as necessary, roll out the dough into a 12- by 9-inch (30 by 23 cm) oval. Lightly flour any sticky places on the dough. The dough should feel soft and smooth all over, but not at all sticky.

2 Sprinkle the cornmeal on the baking sheet and place the dough oval on the cornmeal. Using the handle of a wooden spoon, dimple the flatbread at 2-inch (5 cm) intervals.

3 Spread the caramelized shallots and garlic over the top of the flatbread, then sprinkle with rosemary.

4 Cover with a tea towel and let rest at room temperature for 40 minutes.

5 About 30 minutes before baking, place the broiler pan on the lower shelf and the baking stone on the middle shelf of the oven. Preheat to 450°F (230°C).

6 Carefully pull the middle rack of the oven out several inches. Place the baking sheet on the hot stone. Push the middle rack back in place. Pull the lower rack out, pour the hot water into the broiler pan and push the lower rack back in place. Close the oven door immediately so the steam will envelop the oven.

7 Bake for 20 to 25 minutes or until the crust is lightly browned. Transfer to a wire rack to cool.

White Whole Wheat Pizza with Grilled Vegetables

Makes 1 pizza, to serve 4

This artisan-style pizza features a crisp whole-grain crust and simple grilled toppings, but it can be customized with the toppings of your choice.

INGREDIENTS

$\frac{1}{4}$ recipe prepared Easy Artisan Whole-Grain Dough (page 54), about the size of a softball, made with white whole wheat flour

Unbleached all-purpose or bread flour

1 cup (250 mL) chopped tomatoes

1 cup (250 mL) chopped grilled vegetables, such as onion, zucchini and bell pepper

$\frac{1}{2}$ cup (125 mL) freshly grated Parmesan or shredded Asiago cheese

2 tbsp (25 mL) olive oil

2 cups (500 mL) hot water

1 cup (250 mL) packed baby arugula

EQUIPMENT

Rolling pin

12-inch (30 cm) round perforated pizza pan

Broiler pan

Baking stone

METHOD

1 Place dough on a floured surface and dust very lightly with flour. Flour your hands and the rolling pin. Working the dough as little as possible and adding flour as necessary, roll out the dough into a 12-inch (30 cm) circle. Lightly flour any sticky places on the dough as you roll. The dough should feel gently taut and smooth all over, but not at all sticky.

2 Drape the dough over the rolling pin and transfer to the pizza pan. Pat into place. Cover with a tea towel and let rest at room temperature for 40 minutes.

3 About 30 minutes before baking, place the broiler pan on the lower shelf and the baking stone on the middle shelf of the oven. Preheat to 450°F (230°C).

4 Sprinkle tomatoes, grilled vegetables and Parmesan over the dough, then drizzle with olive oil.

5 Place the pizza pan on the hot stone. Pull the lower rack out, pour the hot water into the broiler pan and push the lower rack back in place. Close the oven door immediately so the steam will envelop the oven.

6 Bake for 15 minutes or until the edges of the crust have browned. Place the arugula in the center of the pizza. To serve, cut the pizza into wedges.

SUGGESTIONS

This type of thin-crust pizza is not meant for heavy sauce, cheese and meat toppings. Instead, use toppings that add bold flavor without bulk, such as thinly sliced onion, prosciutto or crisp-cooked pancetta, grated aged cheeses, chèvre, feta or blue cheese crumbles, olives, pesto, roasted red pepper, cooked Italian sausage crumbles, thinly sliced mushrooms, fresh herbs, fresh tomatoes, oil-packed sun-dried tomatoes or thin asparagus stalks.

VARIATION

You can also use Easy Artisan Dough (page 36) or Easy Artisan Whole-Grain Dough made with semolina or whole wheat flour.

Easy Artisan Seeded and Filled Dough

Makes enough dough for bread, rolls, pizza or flatbread to serve 12 to 16

Adding a coating or filling to a prepared dough is the next step in making artisan breads. Once you've mastered this step — which is more about a new technique than a new recipe — you can customize just about any dough with your own fillings or coatings. Instead of a moist inner filling that is spread on the dough, these dry filling ingredients will be dispersed throughout the dough with a rolling pin. For the outer coating, you'll brush a loaf with lightly beaten egg white, then sprinkle and pat on the topping. The topping on the bread usually either hints at its flavor (grated cheese, rolled oats, herbs) or is decorative (seeds).

INGREDIENTS

½ recipe prepared Easy Artisan Dough (page 36), about the size of a volleyball

Unbleached all-purpose or bread flour

½ cup (125 mL) cornmeal

Filling

1 cup (250 mL) dried fruit, snipped into small pieces, toasted chopped nuts, chopped oil-cured olives, dried or chopped fresh herbs and/or seeds

Topping

1 egg white, lightly beaten

½ cup (125 mL) seeds, such as sesame, poppy, fennel, nigella or a mixture

EQUIPMENT

Rolling pin

Three-sided cookie sheet, flexible cutting board or baker's peel

METHOD

1 Place dough on a floured surface and dust very lightly with flour. Flour your hands and the rolling pin. Working the dough as little as possible and adding flour as necessary, roll out the dough into a 16-inch (40 cm) long oval. Sprinkle one-quarter of the filling on the upper half of the dough oval and press into the dough with your hands. Fold the other half over the filling. Turn the dough a quarter turn. Working the dough as little as possible and adding flour as necessary, roll out the dough into an oval. Sprinkle another quarter of the filling on the upper half of the oval and press into the dough with your hands. Fold the other half over the filling. Turn the dough a quarter turn. Working the dough as little as possible and adding flour as necessary, roll out the dough into an oval. Repeat this process twice more, until all of the filling has been incorporated into the dough.

2 Use that day or place the dough, covered with plastic wrap, in the refrigerator for up to 3 days before baking.

VARIATION

You can also use Easy Artisan Whole-Grain Dough (page 56) or Easy Artisan Flavored Dough (page 92.)

SEED	HOW USED	FLAVOR
Anise	Rolled into dough	Licorice
Caraway	Rolled into dough; patted on crust	Caraway
Cardamom	Crushed, stirred into sweet dough	Cardamom
Cumin	Rolled into dough; patted on crust	Cumin
Dill	Rolled into dough; patted on crust	Dill
Fennel	Rolled into dough; patted on crust	Licorice
Pepita (pumpkin)	Patted on crust	Nutty
Poppy	Rolled into dough; patted on crust	Sweet
Millet	Rolled into dough; patted on crust	Mildly nutty
Nigella	Rolled into dough; patted on crust	Onion
Sesame	Patted on crust	Sesame
Sunflower	Rolled into dough; patted on crust	Nutty

Sesame Semolina Boule

Makes 1 large round loaf, or boule, to serve 8

This classic artisan loaf has a slightly more honeycombed crumb and mellow yellow color — from the high-protein semolina flour — as well as a patterned crust from the sesame seeds.

INGREDIENTS

½ recipe prepared Easy Artisan Whole-Grain Dough (page 54), about the size of a volleyball, made with semolina

Unbleached all-purpose or bread flour

½ cup (125 mL) cornmeal

1 egg white, lightly beaten

½ cup (125 mL) sesame seeds

2 cups (500 mL) hot water

EQUIPMENT

Three-sided cookie sheet, flexible cutting board or baker's peel

Broiler pan

Baking stone

METHOD

1 Place dough on a floured surface and dust very lightly with flour. Flour your hands. Working the dough as little as possible and adding flour as necessary, form the dough into a 12-inch (30 cm) round. Smooth the dough with your hands to form a soft, non-sticky skin. Pinch any seams together. Lightly flour any sticky places on the dough. The dough should feel soft and smooth all over, but not at all sticky.

2 Sprinkle the cornmeal on the cookie sheet and place the dough round on the cornmeal. Cover with a tea towel and let rest at room temperature for 40 minutes.

3 About 30 minutes before baking, place the broiler pan on the lower shelf and the baking stone on the middle shelf of the oven. Preheat to 450°F (230°C).

4 Brush the boule with egg white. Sprinkle and pat on the seeds.

5 Using a serrated knife, make three evenly spaced slashes, about 1 inch (2.5 cm) deep, across the boule, exposing the moist dough under the surface.

6 Carefully pull the middle rack of the oven out several inches. Hold the cutting board level with the rack so that the dough round will slide onto the center of the hot stone. With a quick forward jerk of your arms, slide the dough round from the cookie sheet to the stone. Push the middle rack back in place. Pull the lower rack out, pour the hot water into the broiler pan and push the lower rack back in place. Close the oven door immediately so the steam will envelop the oven.

7 Bake for 27 to 30 minutes or until the crust is a medium dark brown and an instant-read thermometer inserted in the center of the loaf registers at least 190°F (90°C). Remove the loaf to cool on a wire rack.

Oatmeal Honey Boule

Use Oatmeal Honey Dough (page 59) and top with ½ cup (125 mL) rolled oats.

Italian Asiago Boule

Substitute coarsely shredded Asiago for the Cheddar.

Whole Wheat Cheddar Boule

Makes 1 large round loaf, or boule, to serve 8

For maximum flavor, use an aged Cheddar to stand up to the robust whole wheat. You'll fill and top this bread with cheese.

INGREDIENTS

½ recipe prepared Easy Artisan Whole-Grain Dough (page 54), about the size of a volleyball, made with semolina

Unbleached all-purpose or bread flour

1½ cups (375 mL) shredded aged Cheddar cheese

½ cup (125 mL) cornmeal

1 egg white, lightly beaten

2 cups (500 mL) hot water

EQUIPMENT

Rolling pin

Three-sided cookie sheet, flexible cutting board or baker's peel

Broiler pan

Baking stone

METHOD

1 Place dough on a floured surface and dust very lightly with flour. Flour your hands and the rolling pin. Working the dough as little as possible and adding flour as necessary, roll out the dough into a 16-inch (40 cm) long oval. Reserve 2 tbsp (25 mL) of the cheese for topping. Sprinkle one-quarter of the remaining cheese on the upper half of the dough oval and press into the dough with your hands. Fold the other half over the cheese. Turn the dough a quarter turn. Working the dough as little as possible and adding flour as necessary, roll out the dough into an oval. Sprinkle another quarter of the cheese on the upper half of the oval and press into the dough with your hands. Fold the other half over the cheese. Turn the dough a quarter turn. Working the dough as little as possible and adding flour as necessary, roll out the dough into an oval. Repeat this process twice more, until of the cheese has been incorporated into the dough.

2 Working the dough as little as possible and adding flour as necessary, form the dough into a 12-inch (30 cm) round. Smooth the dough with your hands to form a soft, non-sticky skin. Pinch any seams together. Lightly flour any sticky places on the dough. The dough should feel soft and smooth all over, but not at all sticky.

3 Sprinkle the cornmeal on the cookie sheet and place the dough round on the cornmeal. Cover with a tea towel and let rest at room temperature for 40 minutes.

4 About 30 minutes before baking, place the broiler pan on the lower shelf and the baking stone on the middle shelf of the oven. Preheat to 450°F (230°C).

5 Brush the boule with egg white. Sprinkle and pat on the reserved cheese.

6 Using a serrated knife, make three evenly spaced slashes, about 1 inch (2.5 cm) deep, across the boule, exposing the moist dough under the surface.

7 Carefully pull the middle rack of the oven out several inches. Hold the cutting board level with the rack so that the dough round will slide onto the center of the hot stone. With a quick forward jerk of your arms, slide the dough round from the cookie sheet to the stone. Push the middle rack back in place. Pull the lower rack out, pour the hot water into the broiler pan and push the lower rack back in place. Close the oven door immediately so the steam will envelop the oven.

8 Bake for 27 to 30 minutes or until the crust is a medium dark brown and an instant-read thermometer inserted in the center of the loaf registers at least 190°F (90°C). Remove the loaf to cool on a wire rack.

Rosemary Walnut Boule

Makes 1 large round loaf, or boule, to serve 8

Rosemary Walnuts (page 195) are delicious for snacking, but are equally good as a filling for artisan bread.

INGREDIENTS

½ recipe prepared Easy Artisan Dough (page 36), about the size of a volleyball

Unbleached all-purpose or bread flour

½ recipe Rosemary Walnuts (page 195), coarsely chopped

½ cup (125 mL) cornmeal

2 cups (500 mL) hot water

EQUIPMENT

Rolling pin

Three-sided cookie sheet, flexible cutting board or baker's peel

Broiler pan

Baking stone

METHOD

1 Place dough on a floured surface and dust very lightly with flour. Flour your hands and the rolling pin. Working the dough as little as possible and adding flour as necessary, roll out the dough into a 16-inch (40 cm) long oval. Sprinkle one-quarter of the walnuts on the upper half of the dough oval and press into the dough with your hands. Fold the other half over the walnuts. Turn the dough a quarter turn. Working the dough as little as possible and adding flour as necessary, roll out the dough into an oval. Sprinkle another quarter of the walnuts on the upper half of the oval and press into the dough with your hands. Fold the other half over the walnuts. Turn the dough a quarter turn. Working the dough as little as possible and adding flour as necessary, roll out the dough into an oval. Repeat this process twice more, until all of the walnuts have been incorporated into the dough.

2 Working the dough as little as possible and adding flour as necessary, form the dough into a 10-inch (25 cm) round. Smooth the dough with your hands to form a soft, non-sticky skin. Pinch any seams together. Lightly flour any sticky places on the dough. The dough should feel soft and smooth all over, but not at all sticky.

3 Sprinkle the cornmeal on the cookie sheet and place the dough round on the cornmeal. Cover with a tea towel and let rest at room temperature for 40 minutes.

4 About 30 minutes before baking, place the broiler pan on the lower shelf and the baking stone on the middle shelf of the oven. Preheat to 450°F (230°C).

5 Using a serrated knife, make three evenly spaced slashes, about ½ inch (1 cm) deep, across the boule, exposing the moist dough under the surface.

6 Carefully pull the middle rack of the oven out several inches. Hold the cutting board level with the rack so that the dough round will slide onto the center of the hot stone. With a quick forward jerk of your arms, slide the dough round from the cookie sheet to the stone. Push the middle rack back in place. Pull the lower rack out, pour the hot water into the broiler pan and push the lower rack back in place. Close the oven door immediately so the steam will envelop the oven.

7 Bake for 27 to 30 minutes or until the crust is a medium dark brown and an instant-read thermometer inserted in the center of the loaf registers at least 190°F (90°C). Remove the loaf to cool on a wire rack.

VARIATION

You can also use Easy Artisan Whole-Grain Dough (page 54). Make the slashes 1 inch (2.5 cm) deep.

Orchard Batard

Makes 1 large loaf, to serve 8 to 10

Filled with succulent dried fruit, this bread is delicious toasted, spread with cream cheese and drizzled with wildflower or clover honey. There is no topping, but the brush of egg white produces a glistening crust.

INGREDIENTS

$\frac{1}{2}$ recipe prepared Easy Artisan Dough (page 34), about the size of a volleyball

Unbleached all-purpose or bread flour

1 cup (250 mL) mixed dried fruit, such as snipped apricots, figs, dates, dried cherries and golden raisins

$\frac{1}{2}$ cup (50 mL) cornmeal

1 egg white, lightly beaten

2 cups (500 mL) hot water

EQUIPMENT

Rolling pin

Three-sided cookie sheet

Flexible cutting board, floured, or two metal spatulas

Broiler pan

Baking stone

METHOD

1 Place dough on a floured surface and dust very lightly with flour. Flour your hands and the rolling pin. Working the dough as little as possible and adding flour as necessary, roll out the dough into a 16-inch (40 cm) long oval. Sprinkle one-quarter of the fruit on the upper half of the dough oval and press into the dough with your hands. Fold the other half over the fruit. Turn the dough a quarter turn. Working the dough as little as possible and adding flour as necessary, roll out the dough into an oval. Sprinkle another quarter of the fruit on the upper half of the oval and press into the dough with your hands. Fold the other half over the fruit. Turn the dough a quarter turn. Working the dough as little as possible and adding flour as necessary, roll out the dough into an oval. Repeat this process twice more, until all of the fruit has been incorporated into the dough.

2 Working the dough as little as possible and adding flour as necessary, form the dough into a 14-inch (35 cm) cylinder. Pinch the ends and any seams closed. Lightly flour any sticky places on the dough. The dough should feel soft and smooth all over, but not at all sticky.

3 Sprinkle the cornmeal on the cookie sheet. Using the cutting board or two metal spatulas, transfer the loaf to the cookie sheet. Cover with a tea towel and let rest at room temperature for 40 minutes.

4 About 30 minutes before baking, place the broiler pan on the lower shelf and the baking stone on the middle shelf of the oven. Preheat to 450°F (230°C).

5 Brush the batard with egg white.

6 Using a serrated knife, make five cross-hatch slashes, about $\frac{1}{2}$ inch (1 cm) deep, diagonally across the top of the loaf, exposing the moist dough across the top of the loaf, exposing the moist dough inside.

7 Carefully pull the middle rack of the oven out several inches. Hold the cookie sheet level with the rack so that the loaf will slide sideways onto the hot stone. With a quick forward jerk of your arms, slide the loaf from the cookie sheet to the stone. If necessary, use a metal spatula to reposition the loaf. Push the middle rack back in place. Pull the lower rack out, pour the hot water into the broiler pan and push the lower rack back in place. Close the oven door immediately so the steam will envelop the oven.

8 Bake for 25 to 27 minutes or until the crust is dark brown and an instant-read thermometer inserted in the center registers at least 190°F (90°C). Remove the loaf to cool on a wire rack.

Fougasse aux Grattons

Makes 1 flatbread, to serve 4 to 6

This one would be delicious as an appetizer with a cocktail or glass of wine, with a hearty soup, with a brunch casserole or, as they do in Provence, with a bitter green salad of endive or dandelion greens. Best served warm.

INGREDIENTS

$\frac{1}{2}$ cup (125 mL) dry white wine

8 slices smoked bacon or 8 oz (250 g) pancetta, finely chopped

$\frac{1}{4}$ recipe prepared Easy Artisan Dough (page 36), about the size of a softball

2 cups (500 mL) hot water

EQUIPMENT

Rolling pin

Large baking sheet, lined with parchment paper

Broiler pan

Baking stone

METHOD

1 In a skillet, bring wine and bacon to a boil over medium heat. Reduce heat to low and simmer for 35 to 40 minutes or until the fat is rendered and bacon is browned. Using a slotted spoon, transfer bacon to a plate lined with paper towels to drain. Reserve the melted fat in the skillet.

2 Place dough on a floured surface and dust very lightly with flour. Flour your hands and the rolling pin. Working the dough as little as possible and adding flour as necessary, roll out the dough into a 12- by 6-inch (30 by 15 cm) oval. Lightly flour any sticky places on the dough. The dough should feel soft and smooth all over, but not at all sticky.

3 Arrange one-quarter of the grattons on the upper half of the dough and press into the dough with your hands. Fold the other half over the grattons. Turn the dough a quarter turn. Working the dough as little as possible and adding flour as necessary, roll out the dough into an oval. Arrange another quarter of the grattons on the upper half of the dough and press into the dough with your hands. Fold the other half over the grattons. Turn the dough a quarter turn. Working the dough as little as possible and adding flour as necessary, roll out the dough into an oval. Repeat this process twice more, until all of the grattons have been incorporated into the dough.

4 Using a pizza wheel or a sharp knife, cut two rows of four diagonal slashes evenly spaced along the length of the oval, about 2 to 3 inches (5 to 7.5 cm) long, that almost meet in the middle of the dough, like this: /\. Transfer the dough to the prepared baking sheet and pull the top and sides of the dough to stretch it into a larger oval with opened slits. Brush the surface of the dough with the melted bacon fat.

5 Cover with a tea towel and let rest at room temperature for 40 minutes.

6 About 30 minutes before baking, place the broiler pan on the lower shelf and the baking stone on the middle shelf of the oven. Preheat to 450°F (230°C).

7 Carefully pull the middle rack of the oven out several inches. Place the baking sheet on the hot stone. Push the middle rack back in place. Pull the lower rack out, pour the hot water into the broiler pan and push the lower rack back in place. Close the oven door immediately so the steam will envelop the oven.

8 Bake for 22 to 25 minutes or until the crust is medium brown. Transfer to a wire rack to cool.

Rosemary and Black Olive Fougasse

Makes 1 flatbread, to serve 4 to 6

Pair this savory fougasse with a rich Burgundy or Merlot.

INGREDIENTS

1 cup (250 mL) chopped oil-cured pitted black olives

1 tbsp (15 mL) fresh rosemary leaves

$\frac{1}{4}$ recipe prepared Easy Artisan Dough (page 36), about the size of a softball

Olive oil

2 cups (500 mL) hot water

EQUIPMENT

Rolling pin

Large baking sheet, lined with parchment paper

Broiler pan

Baking stone

METHOD

1 In a bowl, combine olives and rosemary.

2 Place dough on a floured surface and dust very lightly with flour. Flour your hands and the rolling pin. Working the dough as little as possible and adding flour as necessary, roll out the dough into a 12- by 6-inch (30 by 15 cm) oval. Lightly flour any sticky places on the dough. The dough should feel soft and smooth all over, but not at all sticky.

3 Arrange one-quarter of the filling on the upper half of the dough and press into the dough with your hands. Fold the other half over the filling. Turn the dough a quarter turn. Working the dough as little as possible and adding flour as necessary, roll out the dough into an oval. Arrange another quarter of the filling on the upper half of the dough and press into the dough with your hands. Fold the other half over the filling. Turn the dough a quarter turn. Working the dough as little as possible and adding flour as necessary, roll out the dough into an oval. Repeat this process twice more, until all of the filling has been incorporated into the dough.

4 Using a pizza wheel or a sharp knife, cut two rows of four diagonal slashes evenly spaced along the length of the oval, about 2 to 3 inches (5 to 7.5 cm) long, that almost meet in the middle of the dough, like this: /\. Transfer the dough to the prepared baking sheet and pull the top and sides of the dough to stretch it into a larger oval with opened slits. Brush the surface of the dough with olive oil.

5 Cover with a tea towel and let rest at room temperature for 40 minutes.

6 About 30 minutes before baking, place the broiler pan on the lower shelf and the baking stone on the middle shelf of the oven. Preheat to 450°F (230°C).

7 Carefully pull the middle rack of the oven out several inches. Place the baking sheet on the hot stone. Push the middle rack back in place. Pull the lower rack out, pour the hot water into the broiler pan and push the lower rack back in place. Close the oven door immediately so the steam will envelop the oven.

8 Bake for 22 to 25 minutes or until the crust is medium brown. Transfer to a wire rack to cool.

Peshawari Naan

Makes 8 flatbreads

Peshawar is a city in northern Pakistan just east of Kabul, Afghanistan, and the Khyber Pass. It's a town known for its naan stuffed with locally grown goodies — different kinds of raisins, herbs and roasted nuts such as pistachios, almonds and cashews.

INGREDIENTS

1 tbsp (15 mL) roasted salted cashews

1 tbsp (15 mL) roasted salted pistachios

1 tbsp (15 mL) golden raisins

1 tsp (5 mL) fennel seeds

$\frac{1}{4}$ recipe prepared Traditional Naan Dough (page 60), about the size of a softball

Unbleached all-purpose or bread flour

$\frac{1}{4}$ cup (50 mL) cornmeal

Melted butter or olive oil

2 cups (500 mL) hot water

EQUIPMENT

Rolling pin

Large baking sheet

Broiler pan

Baking stone

Metal spatula

METHOD

1 In a food processor or mini chopper, combine cashews, pistachios, raisins and fennel seeds; process until finely ground.

2 Place dough on a floured surface and dust very lightly with flour. Flour your hands and the rolling pin. Working the dough as little as possible and adding flour as necessary, form the dough into an 8-inch (20 cm) cylinder. With a dough scraper, cut the dough into 1-inch (2.5 cm) slices. Roll out each slice into a 6-inch (15 cm) long oval. Lightly flour any sticky places on the dough. The dough should feel soft and smooth all over, but not at all sticky.

3 Sprinkle one-eighth of the filling on the upper half of each dough oval and press into the dough with your hands. Fold the other half over the filling. Turn the dough a quarter turn. Working the dough as little as possible and adding flour as necessary, roll out the dough into a 6-inch (15 cm) oval.

4 Sprinkle the cornmeal on the baking sheet and place the dough ovals on the cornmeal. Cover with a tea towel and let rest at room temperature for 40 minutes.

5 About 30 minutes before baking, place the broiler pan on the lower shelf and the baking stone on the middle shelf of the oven. Preheat to 450°F (230°C).

6 Brush with melted butter. Brush the naan with melted butter.

7 Place naan on baking stone and add water to broiler pan. Carefully pull the middle rack of the oven out several inches. With a metal spatula, place four naan on the hot stone. Pull the lower rack out, pour the hot water into the broiler pan and push the lower rack back in place. Close the oven door immediately so the steam will envelop the oven.

8 Bake for 7 to 8 minutes or until the crust is lightly blistered. Remove the naan to cool on a wire rack. Repeat the baking process with the remaining naan.

TIP

Look for maida, atta and other naan ingredients at Indian grocers.

Grilled Peshawari Naan

Prepare a hot fire in your barbecue grill or heat a ridged grill pan indoors. Brush both sides of the naan with melted butter or olive oil and grill, turning once, until they have good grill marks, about 1 minute per side.

Easy Artisan Flavored Dough

Makes enough dough for bread, rolls, pizza or flatbread to serve 12 to 16

In this master recipe, we substitute flavoring liquids for some of the water and stir in dried herbs, spices and other boldly flavored ingredients to create customized breads.

INGREDIENTS

6½ cups (1.625 L) unbleached all-purpose or bread flour

2 tbsp (25 mL) instant or bread machine yeast

1½ tbsp (22 mL) fine kosher salt

Dried herbs, spices or other flavoring ingredients (optional, see page 93 for suggestions and amounts)

3 to 4 cups (750 mL to 1 L) lukewarm liquid (see tip), about 100°F (38°C)

EQUIPMENT

Instant-read thermometer

16-cup (4 L) mixing bowl

Wooden spoon or Danish dough whisk

METHOD

1 Spoon the flour into a measuring cup, level with a knife or your finger, then dump the flour into the mixing bowl.

2 Add the yeast and salt to the flour. Add optional ingredients, if desired. Stir together with a wooden spoon or Danish dough whisk. Pour in the liquids and stir together until just moistened. Beat 40 strokes, scraping the bottom and the sides of the bowl, until the dough forms a lumpy, sticky mass.

3 Cover the bowl with plastic wrap and let rise at room temperature (72°F/22°C) in a draft-free place for 2 hours or until the dough has risen nearly to the top of the bowl and has a sponge-like appearance.

4 Use that day or place the dough, covered with plastic wrap, in the refrigerator for up to 3 days before baking.

TIPS

- For the liquid component, you can use milk, buttermilk, beer, juice, applesauce or puréed squash or pumpkin in addition to water. Milk, juice and beer can be substituted 1 cup for 1 cup (250 mL) for up to 2 cups (750 mL) of the water, keeping the total liquid at 3 cups (750 mL). The puréed squash and pumpkin, applesauce and buttermilk are more dense, so you can replace them 1 cup for 1 cup (250 mL) for up to 2 cups (500 mL) of the water, but to compensate, you'll need to stir in additional water to equal 4 cups (1 L) liquid. You can also add up to ¼ cup (50 mL) liquid honey without decreasing the amount of the other liquids.
- Before storing the dough in the refrigerator, use a permanent marker to write the date on the plastic wrap, so you'll know when you made your dough — and when to use it up 3 days later.

BAKING WITH CANADIAN BREAD FLOUR

Canadian bread flour generally has a higher protein content than U.S. bread flour. That means it absorbs more water. If using Canadian bread flour, you may need to use slightly more water to avoid a dry dough. Begin by adding an extra tablespoon or two (15 to 30 mL) of water and continue adding until a soft dough is formed.

EASY ARTISAN FLAVORED BREADS IN MINUTES A DAY

Day 1: Stir the dough together and let rise. Bake, or cover and chill.

Days 2–3: Remove part of the dough, form and bake.

FLAVORING	AMOUNT TO ADD	HOW TO USE
Chocolate chips	1 to 2 cups (250 to 500 mL)	Stir into flour mixture
Citrus zest or oil	1 to 2 tsp (5 to 10 mL)	Stir into liquid ingredients
Dried fruits	1 to 2 cups (250 to 500 mL)	Steep in liquid ingredients for 15 minutes
Herbs, dried	1 to 2 tbsp (15 to 25 mL)	Stir into flour mixture
Garlic, roasted and mashed	Up to 1 bulb	Stir into flour mixture
Onion, chopped and sautéed	1 cup (250 mL)	Stir into flour mixture or fold into dough after it has risen
Pesto	1 cup (250 mL)	Fold into dough after it has risen
Saffron	1 to 2 tsp (5 to 10 mL)	Steep in liquid ingredients for 30 minutes
Seeds	1 cup (250 mL)	Stir into flour mixture or fold into dough after it has risen
Spices	1 to 2 tbsp (15 to 25 mL)	Stir into flour mixture
Sun-dried tomatoes	$\frac{1}{2}$ cup (125 mL)	Finely chop and stir into liquid ingredients

Brewhouse Dough

Makes enough dough for bread, rolls, pizza or flatbread to serve 12 to 16

Breads made from this dough are delicious with artisan cheeses and charcuterie.

INGREDIENTS

$6\frac{1}{2}$ cups (1.625 L) unbleached all-purpose or bread flour

2 tbsp (25 mL) instant or bread machine yeast

$1\frac{1}{2}$ tbsp (22 mL) fine kosher salt

2 cups (500 mL) good-quality good quality beer, either lager or ale

1 cup (250 mL) hot water

$\frac{1}{4}$ cup (50 mL) liquid honey

EQUIPMENT

Instant-read thermometer

16-cup (4 L) mixing bowl

Wooden spoon or Danish dough whisk

4-cup (1 L) glass measuring cup

METHOD

1 Spoon the flour into a measuring cup, level with a knife or your finger, then dump the flour into the mixing bowl.

2 Add the yeast and salt to the flour. Stir together with a wooden spoon or Danish dough whisk. In the glass measuring cup, combine beer, hot water and honey. Pour into the flour mixture and stir together until just moistened. Beat 40 strokes, scraping the bottom and the sides of the bowl, until the dough forms a lumpy, sticky mass.

3 Cover the bowl with plastic wrap and let rise at room temperature (72°F/22°C) in a draft-free place for 2 hours or until the dough has risen nearly to the top of the bowl and has a sponge-like appearance.

4 Use that day or place the dough, covered with plastic wrap, in the refrigerator for up to 3 days before baking.

BAKING WITH CANADIAN BREAD FLOUR

Canadian bread flour generally has a higher protein content than U.S. bread flour. That means it absorbs more water. If using Canadian bread flour, you may need to use slightly more water to avoid a dry dough. Begin by adding an extra tablespoon or two (15 to 30 mL) of water and continue adding until a soft dough is formed.

Shaker Buttermilk Dough

Makes enough dough for bread, rolls, pizza or flatbread to serve 12 to 16

Shaker religious communities throughout the eastern United States were known for the quality of their homemade foods, including this dough.

INGREDIENTS

$6\frac{1}{2}$ cups (1.625 L) unbleached all-purpose or bread flour

2 tbsp (25 mL) instant or bread machine yeast

$1\frac{1}{2}$ tbsp (22 mL) fine kosher salt

2 cups (500 mL) buttermilk

2 cups (500 mL) hot water

EQUIPMENT

Instant-read thermometer

16-cup (4 L) mixing bowl

Wooden spoon or Danish dough whisk

4-cup (1 L) glass measuring cup

METHOD

1 Spoon the flour into a measuring cup, level with a knife or your finger, then dump the flour into the mixing bowl.

2 Add the yeast and salt to the flour. Stir together with a wooden spoon or Danish dough whisk. In the glass measuring cup, combine buttermilk and hot water. Pour into the flour mixture and stir together until just moistened. Beat 40 strokes, scraping the bottom and the sides of the bowl, until the dough forms a lumpy, sticky mass.

3 Cover the bowl with plastic wrap and let rise at room temperature (72°F/22°C) in a draft-free place for 2 hours or until the dough has risen nearly to the top of the bowl and has a sponge-like appearance.

4 Use that day or place the dough, covered with plastic wrap, in the refrigerator for up to 3 days before baking.

BAKING WITH CANADIAN BREAD FLOUR

Canadian bread flour generally has a higher protein content than U.S. bread flour. That means it absorbs more water. If using Canadian bread flour, you may need to use slightly more water to avoid a dry dough. Begin by adding an extra tablespoon or two (15 to 30 mL) of water and continue adding until a soft dough is formed.

Hamburger Bun Dough

Makes enough dough for buns to serve 12 to 16

The addition of sugar and milk to the dough makes a soft bun with a good crust.

INGREDIENTS

$6\frac{1}{2}$ cups (1.625 L) unbleached all-purpose or bread flour

2 tbsp (25 mL) instant or bread machine yeast

$1\frac{1}{2}$ tbsp (22 mL) fine kosher salt

1 cup (250 mL) granulated sugar

$1\frac{1}{2}$ cups (375 mL) 2% milk

$1\frac{1}{2}$ cups (375 mL) hot water

EQUIPMENT

Instant-read thermometer

16-cup (4 L) mixing bowl

Wooden spoon or Danish dough whisk

4-cup (1 L) glass measuring cup

METHOD

1 Spoon the flour into a measuring cup, level with a knife or your finger, then dump the flour into the mixing bowl.

2 Add the yeast and salt to the flour. Stir together with a wooden spoon or Danish dough whisk. In the glass measuring cup, combine sugar, milk and hot water. Pour into the flour mixture and stir together until just moistened. Beat 40 strokes, scraping the bottom and the sides of the bowl, until the dough forms a lumpy, sticky mass.

3 Cover the bowl with plastic wrap and let rise at room temperature (72°F/22°C) in a draft-free place for 2 hours or until the dough has risen nearly to the top of the bowl and has a sponge-like appearance.

4 Use that day or place the dough, covered with plastic wrap, in the refrigerator for up to 3 days before baking.

Squash or Pumpkin Dough

Makes enough dough for bread, rolls, pizza or flatbread to serve 12 to 16

Enjoy Thanksgiving leftovers on bread made with this dough.

INGREDIENTS

$6\frac{1}{2}$ cups (1.625 L) unbleached all-purpose or bread flour

2 tbsp (25 mL) instant or bread machine yeast

$1\frac{1}{2}$ tbsp (22 mL) fine kosher salt

2 cups (500 mL) puréed cooked squash or pumpkin

2 cups (500 mL) hot water

$\frac{1}{4}$ cup (50 mL) liquid honey

1 tbsp (15 mL) pumpkin pie spice

EQUIPMENT

Instant-read thermometer

16-cup (4 L) mixing bowl

Wooden spoon or Danish dough whisk

4-cup (1 L) glass measuring cup

METHOD

1 Spoon the flour into a measuring cup, level with a knife or your finger, then dump the flour into the mixing bowl.

2 Add the yeast and salt to the flour. Stir together with a wooden spoon or Danish dough whisk. In the glass measuring cup, combine squash, hot water, honey and pumpkin pie spice. Pour into the flour mixture and stir together until just moistened. Beat 40 strokes, scraping the bottom and the sides of the bowl, until the dough forms a lumpy, sticky mass.

3 Cover the bowl with plastic wrap and let rise at room temperature (72°F/22°C) in a draft-free place for 2 hours or until the dough has risen nearly to the top of the bowl and has a sponge-like appearance.

4 Use that day or place the dough, covered with plastic wrap, in the refrigerator for up to 3 days before baking.

Sun-Dried Tomato Dough

Makes enough dough for bread, rolls, pizza or flatbread to serve 12 to 16

Adding sun-dried tomatoes to dough is an easy way to get vibrant color and flavor.

INGREDIENTS

6½ cups (1.625 L) unbleached all-purpose or bread flour

2 tbsp (25 mL) instant or bread machine yeast

1½ tbsp (22 mL) fine kosher salt

3 cups (750 mL) hot water

½ cup (125 mL) snipped oil-packed sun-dried tomatoes

EQUIPMENT

Instant-read thermometer

16-cup (4 L) mixing bowl

Wooden spoon or Danish dough whisk

4-cup (1 L) glass measuring cup

METHOD

1 Spoon the flour into a measuring cup, level with a knife or your finger, then dump the flour into the mixing bowl.

2 Add the yeast and salt to the flour. Stir together with a wooden spoon or Danish dough whisk. In the glass measuring cup, combine hot water, tomatoes and their oil. Pour into the flour mixture and stir together until just moistened. Beat 40 strokes, scraping the bottom and the sides of the bowl, until the dough forms a lumpy, sticky mass.

3 Cover the bowl with plastic wrap and let rise at room temperature (72°F/22°C) in a draft-free place for 2 hours or until the dough has risen nearly to the top of the bowl and has a sponge-like appearance.

4 Use that day or place the dough, covered with plastic wrap, in the refrigerator for up to 3 days before baking.

TIP

Snip the sun-dried tomatoes into small pieces using kitchen shears.

BAKING WITH CANADIAN BREAD FLOUR

Canadian bread flour generally has a higher protein content than U.S. bread flour. That means it absorbs more water. If using Canadian bread flour, you may need to use slightly more water to avoid a dry dough. Begin by adding an extra tablespoon or two (15 to 30 mL) of water and continue adding until a soft dough is formed.

Brewhouse Baguettes

Makes 2 baguettes, to serve 8

These crusty baguettes have tons of flavor from the beer used in place of some of the water in the dough. A touch of honey makes up for the slight bitterness of the brew. These are delicious with hearty soups, aged cheeses, a savory soufflé or beef stew.

INGREDIENTS

$\frac{1}{2}$ recipe prepared Brewhouse Dough (page 94), about the size of a volleyball

Unbleached all-purpose or bread flour

$\frac{1}{2}$ cup (125 mL) cornmeal

2 cups (500 mL) hot water

EQUIPMENT

Three-sided cookie sheet, flexible cutting board or baker's peel

Broiler pan

Baking stone

METHOD

1 Divide the dough in half. Transfer one half to a floured surface and dust very lightly with flour. Flour your hands. Working the dough as little as possible and adding flour as necessary, form the dough into a 14-inch (35 cm) cylinder. Smooth the dough with your hands to form a soft, non-sticky skin. Pinch any seams together. Pinch each end into a point. Lightly flour any sticky places on the dough. The dough should feel soft and smooth all over, but not at all sticky. Repeat with the remaining dough.

2 Sprinkle the cornmeal on the cookie sheet and place baguettes about 6 inches (15 cm) apart on the cornmeal. Cover with tea towels and let rest at room temperature for 40 minutes.

3 About 30 minutes before baking, place the broiler pan on the lower shelf and the baking stone on the middle shelf of the oven. Preheat to 450°F (230°C).

4 Using a serrated knife, make three evenly spaced diagonal slashes, about $\frac{1}{2}$ inch (1 cm) deep, across each baguette, exposing the moist dough under the surface.

5 Carefully pull the middle rack of the oven out several inches. Hold the cookie sheet level with the rack so that the first baguette will slide sideways onto the hot stone. With a quick forward jerk of your arms, slide the first baguette from the cookie sheet to the back of the stone. With another jerk, slide the second baguette onto the front of the stone. Push the middle rack back in place. Pull the lower rack out, pour the hot water into the broiler pan and push the lower rack back in place. Close the oven door immediately so the steam will envelop the oven.

6 Bake for 25 minutes or until the crust is a medium dark brown and an instant-read thermometer inserted in the center of the baguettes registers at least 190°F (90°C). Remove baguettes to cool on a wire rack.

VARIATION

You can also use Easy Artisan Whole-Grain Dough (page 54) or any of its variations. Make the slashes 1 inch (2.5 cm) deep.

Shaker Buttermilk Bread

Makes 2 loaves, to serve 16

A celibate religious sect known for their medicinal herbs, clean-lined architecture and furniture, and the fine table their North American communities kept, the Shakers believed that eating bread hot out of the oven stirred up passions that were best left unstirred. I have to confess, however, that I can't resist the toasty aroma and moist crumb of this bread, still warm and slathered with Artisan Butter (page 198).

INGREDIENTS

½ recipe prepared Shaker Buttermilk Dough (page 96), about the size of a volleyball

Unbleached all-purpose or bread flour

2 cups (500 mL) hot water

EQUIPMENT

Two 9- by 5-inch (23 by 12.5 cm) loaf pans, greased

Broiler pan

Baking stone

Instant-read thermometer

METHOD

1 Divide the dough in half. Transfer one half to a floured surface and dust very lightly with flour. Flour your hands. Working the dough as little as possible and adding flour as necessary, form the dough into an 8-inch (20 cm) cylinder. Smooth the dough with your hands to form a soft, non-sticky skin. Pinch any seams together. Lightly flour any sticky places on the dough. The dough should feel soft and smooth all over, but not at all sticky. Repeat with the remaining dough.

2 Place each cylinder in a prepared loaf pan. Cover with tea towels and let rest at room temperature for 40 minutes.

3 About 30 minutes before baking, place the broiler pan on the lower shelf and the baking stone on the middle shelf of the oven. Preheat to 425°F (220°C).

4 Carefully pull the middle rack of the oven out several inches. Place the loaf pans at least 3 inches (7.5 cm) apart on the hot stone. Push the middle rack back in place. Pull the lower rack out, pour the hot water into the broiler pan and push the lower rack back in place. Close the oven door immediately so the steam will envelop the oven.

5 Bake for 27 to 30 minutes or until the crust is a medium dark brown and an instant-read thermometer inserted in the center of the loaf registers at least 190°F (90°C). Remove from pans and transfer to a wire rack to cool.

Shaker Buttermilk Herb Bread

Stir 2 tbsp (25 mL) dried herbs, such as rosemary, fennel or dillweed, into the dry ingredients when first making the dough.

Orange and Fennel Fougasse

Makes 4 flatbreads, each to serve 4 to 5

In Provence, fougasse is usually a savory flatbread. But it can also be sweet, often flavored with fresh orange zest, orange flower water and fennel. This slightly sweet fougasse is usually baked for Les Treize Desserts (the Thirteen Desserts), part of the Christmas Eve feast. But why not make these, one at a time, as a fabulous hostess or holiday gift from your kitchen?

INGREDIENTS

6½ cups (1.625 L) unbleached all-purpose or bread flour

1½ tbsp (22 mL) instant or bread machine yeast

1½ tbsp (22 mL) fine kosher salt

½ cup (125 mL) granulated sugar

¼ cup (50 mL) fennel seeds

1 tbsp (15 mL) grated orange zest

1 tbsp (15 mL) orange flower water (optional)

3 cups (750 mL) lukewarm water (about 100°F/38°C)

2 tbsp (25 mL) olive oil

2 cups (500 mL) hot water

EQUIPMENT

Instant-read thermometer

16-cup (4 L) mixing bowl

Wooden spoon or Danish dough whisk

Rolling pin

Large baking sheet, lined with parchment paper

Baking stone

Broiler pan

METHOD

1 Spoon the flour into a measuring cup, level with a knife or your finger, then dump the flour into the mixing bowl.

2 Add the yeast and salt to the flour. Add the sugar and fennel seeds. Stir together with a wooden spoon or Danish dough whisk. Add the orange zest and orange flower water to the lukewarm water and stir to combine. Pour into the flour mixture and stir together just until moistened. Beat 40 strokes, scraping the bottom and the sides of the bowl, until the dough forms a lumpy, sticky mass.

3 Cover the bowl with plastic wrap and let rise at room temperature (72°F/22°C) in a draft-free place for 2 hours or until the dough has risen nearly to the top of the bowl and has a sponge-like appearance.

4 Use that day or place the dough, covered with plastic wrap, in the refrigerator for up to 3 days before baking.

5 For each flatbread, remove one-quarter of the dough (about the size of a softball) with a serrated knife and a dough scraper. Transfer the dough to a floured surface and dust very lightly with flour. Flour your hands and the rolling pin. Working the dough as little as possible and adding flour as necessary, roll out the dough into a 12- by 6-inch (30 by 15 cm) oval. Lightly flour any sticky places on the dough. The dough should feel soft and smooth all over, but not at all sticky.

6 Using a pizza wheel or a sharp knife, cut two rows of four diagonal slashes evenly spaced along the length of the oval, about 2 to 3 inches (5 to 7.5 cm) long, that almost meet in the middle of the dough, like this: /\. Transfer the dough to the prepared baking sheet and pull the top and sides of the dough to stretch it into a larger oval with opened slits. Brush the surface of the dough with the olive oil.

7 About 30 minutes before baking, place the broiler pan on the lower shelf and the baking stone on the middle shelf of the oven. Preheat to 450°F (230°C).

8 Carefully pull the middle rack of the oven out several inches. Place the baking sheet on the hot stone. Push the middle rack back in place. Pull the lower rack out, pour the hot water into the broiler pan and push the lower rack back in place. Close the oven door immediately so the steam will envelop the oven.

9 Bake for 17 to 20 minutes or until the crust is medium brown. Transfer to a wire rack to cool.

BAKING WITH CANADIAN BREAD FLOUR

Canadian bread flour generally has a higher protein content than U.S. bread flour. That means it absorbs more water. If using Canadian bread flour, you may need to use slightly more water to avoid a dry dough. Begin by adding an extra tablespoon or two (15 to 30 mL) of water and continue adding until a soft dough is formed.

Mini Hamburger Buns

Makes 32 miniature buns

A little milk and sugar in the dough contribute to a brown crust and a soft crumb, perfect for a juicy lamb, beef or meatball "slider." But why stop there? What about a gourmet sausage, grilled chicken or toasted cheese sandwich? These miniature buns make great cocktail fare — perhaps a Kobe beef burger topped with Easy Caramelized Onions (page 196).

INGREDIENTS

1 recipe prepared Hamburger Bun Dough (page 97)

Unbleached all-purpose or bread flour

1 egg, beaten with 1 tbsp (15 mL) water

2 cups (500 mL) hot water

EQUIPMENT

2 large baking sheets, lined with parchment paper

Broiler pan

Baking stone

METHOD

1 Divide the dough in half. Transfer one half to a floured surface and dust very lightly with flour. Flour your hands. Working the dough as little as possible and adding flour as necessary, form the dough into a 16-inch (40 cm) cylinder. With the dough scraper, slice the cylinder into eight 2-inch (5 cm) pieces. Cut each piece in half. Pinch the cut sides closed and coax each piece into a 2-inch (5 cm) round. Pinch any seams together. Repeat with the remaining dough.

2 Place the buns about 1 inch (2.5 cm) apart on the prepared baking sheets. Cover with tea towels and let rest at room temperature for 40 minutes.

3 About 30 minutes before baking, place the broiler pan on the lower shelf and the baking stone on the middle shelf of the oven. Preheat to 400°F (200°C).

4 Brush the top of each bun with egg wash.

5 Carefully pull the middle rack of the oven out several inches. Place one of the baking sheets on the hot stone. Push the middle rack back in place. Pull the lower rack out, pour the hot water into the broiler pan and push the lower rack back in place. Close the oven door immediately so the steam will envelop the oven.

6 Bake for 15 to 17 minutes or until the buns are domed and lightly browned and an instant-read thermometer inserted in the center of a bun registers at least 190°F (90°C). Remove from pan and transfer to a wire rack to cool. Repeat the baking with the remaining buns.

TIPS

- These rolls are baked at a slightly lower temperature so the tops stay smooth.
- Make the whole batch of rolls, then freeze for up to 3 months in plastic freezer bags.

VARIATION

You can also use any of these other master recipes and all their variations: Easy Artisan Dough (page 36), Easy Artisan Whole-Grain Dough (page 54), Easy Artisan Seeded and Filled Dough (page 76), Easy Artisan Flavored Dough (page 92) or Easy Artisan Slow-Rise Dough (page 110).

Large Hamburger Buns

Slice each cylinder into eight 2-inch (5 cm) pieces and coax each piece into a 4-inch (10 cm) round. Proceed with the recipe. They take the same time to bake, 15 to 17 minutes at 400°F (200°C).

Sun-Dried Tomato and Feta Flatbread

Makes 1 large flatbread, to serve 8 to 12

This golden, puffy flatbread makes a great appetizer or tapas selection, and works well with any casual meal. For even more flavor, and to simulate a Tuscan wood-burning oven, smolder fine wood chips next to the broiler pan as this bakes — a "kiss of smoke" technique often used by barbecuers. If using the wood chips, be sure your kitchen is well ventilated.

INGREDIENTS

½ recipe prepared Sun-Dried Tomato Dough (page 99), about the size of a volleyball

Unbleached all-purpose or bread flour

1 cup (250 mL) prepared basil pesto

8 oz (250 g) feta cheese, crumbled

½ cup (125 mL) chopped fresh flat-leaf (Italian) parsley

Olive oil

2 cups (500 mL) hot water

EQUIPMENT

Rolling pin

Large baking sheet, lined with parchment paper

Broiler pan

Baking stone

¼ cup (50 mL) fine dry hardwood chips, such as mesquite or apple, moistened with 2 tbsp (25 mL) water (optional)

METHOD

1 Place dough on a floured surface and dust very lightly with flour. Flour your hands and the rolling pin. Working the dough as little as possible and adding flour as necessary, roll out the dough into a 12- by 10-inch (30 by 25 cm) rectangle. Lightly flour any sticky places on the dough. The dough should feel soft and smooth all over, but not at all sticky.

2 Transfer the dough to the prepared baking sheet. Spread pesto over the dough. Sprinkle feta and parsley over the pesto, leaving a 1-inch (2.5 cm) perimeter.

3 Cover with a tea towel and let rest at room temperature for 40 minutes.

4 About 30 minutes before baking, place the broiler pan on the lower shelf and the baking stone on the middle shelf of the oven. Preheat to 450°F (230°C). For the wood-burning oven technique, place the moistened wood chips in a small metal pan next to the broiler pan on the lower shelf. They will start to smolder and release wisps of smoke.

5 Drizzle the flatbread with olive oil.

6 Carefully pull the middle rack of the oven out several inches. Place the baking sheet on the hot stone. Push the middle rack back in place. Pull the lower rack out, pour the hot water into the broiler pan and push the lower rack back in place. Close the oven door immediately so the steam will envelop the oven.

7 Bake for 20 to 22 minutes or until the crust is puffed and golden brown. Remove from pan and transfer to a wire rack to cool. Remove the smoldering wood chips from the oven, let cool completely, then discard.

VARIATION

You can also use Easy Artisan Dough (page 36), Easy Artisan Whole-Grain Dough (page 54), made with white whole wheat flour, or Easy Artisan Slow-Rise Dough (page 110).

Easy Artisan Slow-Rise Dough

Makes enough dough for bread, rolls or flatbreads to serve 12 to 16

Decreasing the amount of yeast, adding a starter like a Biga (page 111), and allowing for a longer rising time turns Easy Artisan Dough into a slow-rise dough — and teaches the artisan baker a valuable lesson in patience. Good things come to those who wait. With less yeast and a longer rise, you get a bread with a more developed flavor and the bigger holes of a honeycomb crumb. You also end up with a golden brown, somewhat blistered crust (a hallmark of slow-rise artisan bread). Spraying the loaves with water before and during baking helps promote that blistered crust effect.

This master recipe, which calls for filtered or bottled spring water in the dough because it's more pure than tap water, and this helps the bread rise better. Because of the long, slow rise, the gluten in the flour has more time to make a fibrous network, so the dough will seem moist, yet stringy. And as you work the dough and form the loaves, you'll see and feel air bubbles, part of what will make the honeycomb crumb in the finished bread. This sticky dough is not as easy to divide into small portions, so all the recipes will use half the dough, for larger loaves and flatbreads.

INGREDIENTS

4½ cups (1.125 L) unbleached bread flour

1 cup (250 mL) whole-grain flour (see page 55)

1½ tbsp (22 mL) fine kosher salt

1 recipe prepared Biga (page 111)

3 cups (750 mL) filtered or bottled spring water, at room temperature

EQUIPMENT

16-cup (4 L) mixing bowl

Wooden spoon or Danish dough whisk

METHOD

1 Spoon the flour into a measuring cup, level with a knife or your finger, then dump the flour into the mixing bowl, combining unbleached and whole-grain flours well.

2 Add the salt to the flour. Stir together with a wooden spoon or Danish dough whisk. Add the biga and water and stir together until just moistened. Beat 40 strokes, scraping the bottom and the sides of the bowl, until the dough forms a thick, spongy mass.

3 Cover the bowl with plastic wrap and let ferment at room temperature (72°F/22°C) in a draft-free place for 12 to 18 hours or until it almost reaches the top of the bowl.

4 Use right away or place the bowl, covered with plastic wrap, in the refrigerator for up to 3 days before baking.

TIP

Now that we're in the intermediate phase of artisan bread, we'll switch to a baker's peel. (Of course, you can still use a three-sided cookie sheet or flexible cutting board.)

Biga

Makes about 2 cups (500 mL)

Biga is the Italian name for a pre-ferment, starter or sponge used to make slow-rise breads. You'll mix a tiny amount of yeast with flour and water, then set it aside to ferment at room temperature. After it has fermented, you will add prepared biga to other dough ingredients to make slow-rise bread. Bigas can be thicker or more moist. This one falls in the moister category, so it works with our Easy Artisan Master Dough recipes.

Mix up the biga and let it ferment at room temperature for 6 to 24 hours before making the dough. Biga is an active culture, and it's easy to tell when it's good and when it's not. When it domes in the bowl and you can see bubbles rising and breaking on the surface, it's ready to use. After the biga has domed, cover it and keep it in the refrigerator for up to 3 days before baking. When the biga deflates, its rising power has gone.

INGREDIENTS

3½ cups (875 mL) unbleached all-purpose flour

¼ tsp (1 mL) instant or bread machine yeast

1 cup (250 mL) filtered or bottled spring water, at room temperature

EQUIPMENT

6-cup (1.5 L) bowl

Wooden spoon or Danish dough whisk

METHOD

1 Spoon the flour into a measuring cup, level with a knife or your finger, then dump the flour into a mixing bowl.

2 Add the yeast to the flour. Stir together with a wooden spoon or Danish dough whisk. Pour in the water and stir together until just moistened. Beat 40 strokes, scraping the bottom and the sides of the bowl, until the dough forms a lumpy, sticky mass.

3 Cover the bowl with plastic wrap and let rise at room temperature (72°F/22°C) in a draft-free place for 6 to 24 hours. At first, the biga will look lumpy and shaggy. After several hours, it will look creamy and frothy, with small bubbles that form and rise to the surface. Eventually, it will have a smooth, domed skin, with large, wide bubbles that rise lazily to the surface.

4 Use right away or place the bowl, covered with plastic wrap, in the refrigerator for up to 3 days before baking. If it stays domed, it's ready to go. If it's deflated, it's lost its power, so discard it.

BAKING WITH CANADIAN BREAD FLOUR

Canadian bread flour generally has a higher protein content than U.S. bread flour. That means it absorbs more water. If using Canadian bread flour, you may need to use slightly more water to avoid a dry dough. Begin by adding an extra tablespoon or two (15 to 30 mL) of water and continue adding until a soft dough is formed.

EASY ARTISAN SLOW-RISE BREADS IN MINUTES A DAY

Day 1: Make the biga. Let ferment.

Day 2: Wrap and chill biga or make into a dough.

Days 2–4: Form and rest dough, bake bread.

Slow-Rise Herbed Polenta Dough

Makes enough dough for bread, rolls or flatbreads to serve 12 to 16

Use this pale yellow dough for Tuscan-style breads.

INGREDIENTS

$4\frac{1}{2}$ cups (1.125 L) unbleached bread flour

1 cup (250 mL) cornmeal

$1\frac{1}{2}$ tbsp (22 mL) fine kosher salt

1 tbsp (15 mL) dried rosemary

1 tbsp (15 mL) dried basil

1 recipe prepared Biga (page 150)

3 cups (750 mL) filtered or bottled spring water, at room temperature

EQUIPMENT

16-cup (4 L) mixing bowl

Wooden spoon or Danish dough whisk

METHOD

1 One at a time, spoon the flour and cornmeal into a measuring cup, level with a knife or your finger, then dump into the mixing bowl. Combine well.

2 Add the salt, rosemary and basil to the flour mixture. Stir together with a wooden spoon or Danish dough whisk. Add the biga and water and stir together until just moistened. Beat 40 strokes, scraping the bottom and the sides of the bowl, until the dough forms a thick, spongy mass.

3 Cover the bowl with plastic wrap and let ferment at room temperature (72°F/22°C) in a draft-free place for 12 to 18 hours or until it almost reaches the top of the bowl.

4 Use right away or place the bowl, covered with plastic wrap, in the refrigerator for up to 3 days before baking.

TIP

Because cornmeal doesn't absorb water like other flours, the dough will be very moist.

BAKING WITH CANADIAN BREAD FLOUR

Canadian bread flour generally has a higher protein content than U.S. bread flour. That means it absorbs more water. If using Canadian bread flour, you may need to use slightly more water to avoid a dry dough. Begin by adding an extra tablespoon or two (15 to 30 mL) of water and continue adding until a soft dough is formed.

Slow-Rise Sour Graham Dough

Makes enough dough for bread, rolls or flatbreads to serve 12 to 16

INGREDIENTS

4½ cups (1.125 L) unbleached bread flour

1 cup (250 mL) graham flour (coarsely ground whole wheat)

1½ tbsp (22 mL) fine kosher salt

½ cup (125 mL) non-fat plain yogurt

3 cups (750 mL) filtered or bottled spring water, at room temperature

1 recipe prepared Biga (page 111)

EQUIPMENT

16-cup (4 L) mixing bowl

Wooden spoon or Danish dough whisk

METHOD

1 One at a time, spoon the bread flour and graham flour into a measuring cup, level with a knife or your finger, then dump into the mixing bowl. Combine well.

2 Add the salt to the flours. Stir together with a wooden spoon or Danish dough whisk. Stir yogurt into the water. Pour into the flour mixture, add the biga and stir together until just moistened. Beat 40 strokes, scraping the bottom and the sides of the bowl, until the dough forms a thick, spongy mass.

3 Cover the bowl with plastic wrap and let ferment at room temperature (72°F/22°C) in a draft-free place for 12 to 18 hours or until it almost reaches the top of the bowl.

4 Use right away or place the bowl, covered with plastic wrap, in the refrigerator for up to 3 days before baking.

TIP

Graham flour is available in the specialty baking aisle.

Slow-Rise Rustic French Boule

Makes 1 round loaf, or boule, to serve 6 to 8

Making this classic loaf is a good way to get the feel of the dough and practice patience, as it needs to rest and ferment for 4 hours before baking (you can bake it after a 40-minute rest, but it won't rise as high). This recipe makes a medium-size boule, which will rise dramatically in the oven, producing a crusty loaf with a honeycombed crumb. Spraying the loaf with water contributes to the formation of a medium golden brown, blistered crust. Deliciously easy!

INGREDIENTS

½ recipe prepared Easy Artisan Slow-Rise Dough (page 110), about the size of a volleyball

Unbleached bread flour

½ cup (125 mL) cornmeal (approx.)

2 cups (500 mL) hot water

EQUIPMENT

Baker's peel

Broiler pan

Baking stone

Plastic spray bottle of water

METHOD

1 Place dough on a floured surface and dust very lightly with flour. Flour your hands. Working the dough as little as possible and adding flour as necessary, form the dough into an 8-inch (20 cm) round. Smooth the dough with your hands to form a soft, non-sticky skin. Pinch any seams together. Lightly flour any sticky places on the dough. The dough should feel soft and smooth all over, but not at all sticky.

2 Sprinkle the cornmeal on the baker's peel and place the dough round on the cornmeal. Cover with plastic wrap and let rest at room temperature for 4 hours or until slightly risen.

3 About 30 minutes before baking, place the broiler pan on the lower shelf and the baking stone on the middle shelf of the oven. Preheat to 450°F (230°C).

4 Using a serrated knife, make three evenly spaced slashes, about 1 inch (2.5 cm) deep, across the boule, exposing the moist dough under the surface. With a dough scraper, gently scrape under the boule to make sure it isn't sticking to the peel. Add more cornmeal if necessary.

5 Carefully pull the middle rack of the oven out several inches. Hold the baker's peel level with the rack so that the dough round will slide onto the center of the hot stone. With a quick forward jerk of your arms, slide the dough round from the peel to the stone. Push the middle rack back in place. Pull the lower rack out, pour the hot water into the broiler pan and push the lower rack back in place. Spray the boule with water. Close the oven door immediately so the steam will envelop the oven.

6 Bake for 30 to 32 minutes, spraying the loaf with water three times during baking, until the crust is a blistered medium golden brown and an instant-read thermometer inserted in the center of the loaf registers at least 190°F (90°C). Remove the loaf to cool on a wire rack.

TIP

After baking, keep slow-rise and naturally leavened breads wrapped in a brown paper bag, to keep their crust crisp and their crumb moist.

VARIATION

You can also use Slow-Rise Herbed Polenta Dough (page 112).

Slow-Rise Baguettes

Makes 2 baguettes, to serve 8 to 12

When made with biga, baguettes have a fuller, more developed flavor that is truer to the classic French boulangerie. Spraying the baguette during baking makes for a crisp, blistered crust.

INGREDIENTS

$\frac{1}{2}$ recipe prepared Easy Artisan Slow-Rise Dough (page 110), about the size of a volleyball

Unbleached bread flour

$\frac{1}{2}$ cup (125 mL) cornmeal (approx.)

2 cups (500 mL) hot water

EQUIPMENT

Baker's peel

Broiler pan

Baking stone

Plastic spray bottle of water

METHOD

1 Divide the dough in half. Transfer one half to a floured surface and dust very lightly with flour. Flour your hands. Working the dough as little as possible and adding flour as necessary, form the dough into a 14-inch (35 cm) cylinder. Smooth the dough with your hands to form a soft, non-sticky skin. Pinch any seams together. Pinch each end into a point. Lightly flour any sticky places on the dough. The dough should feel soft and smooth all over, but not at all sticky. Repeat with the remaining dough.

2 Sprinkle the cornmeal on the baker's peel and place the baguettes on the cornmeal, spacing them about 6 inches (15 cm) apart. Cover with plastic wrap and let rest at room temperature for 2 hours or until slightly risen.

3 About 30 minutes before baking, place the broiler pan on the lower shelf and the baking stone on the middle shelf of the oven. Preheat to 450°F (230°C).

4 Using a serrated knife, make three evenly spaced diagonal slashes, about 1 inch (2.5 cm) deep, across each baguette, exposing the moist dough under the surface. With a dough scraper, gently scrape under each baguette to make sure it isn't sticking to the peel. Add more cornmeal, if necessary.

5 Slide baguettes onto baking stone and add water to broiler pan. Carefully pull the middle rack of the oven out several inches. Hold the baker's peel level with the rack so that the first baguette will slide sideways onto the hot stone. With a quick forward jerk of your arms, slide the first baguette from the peel to the back of the stone. With another jerk, slide the second baguette onto the front of the stone. Push the middle rack back in place. Pull the lower rack out, pour the hot water into the broiler pan and push the lower rack back in place. Spray the baguettes with water. Close the oven door immediately so the steam will envelop the oven.

6 Bake for 15 to 17 minutes, spraying the baguettes with water three times during baking, until the crust is a blistered medium golden brown and an instant-read thermometer inserted in the center of the baguettes registers at least 190°F (90°C). Remove baguettes to cool on a wire rack.

VARIATION

You can also use Slow-Rise Herbed Polenta Dough (page 112) or Slow-Rise Sour Graham Dough (page 113).

Slow-Rise Mini Baguettes

Divide the dough in half. Form each half into a 12-inch (30 cm) cylinder. With the dough scraper, cut each cylinder into four 3-inch (7.5 cm) pieces. Form each piece into a baguette and proceed with the recipe. Bake on the stone, in batches, for 12 to 15 minutes.

Rustic Italian Hoagie Rolls

Makes 4 rolls

When you buy great ingredients for a hoagie sandwich, don't forget to make these crusty rolls.

INGREDIENTS

$\frac{1}{2}$ recipe prepared Easy Artisan Slow-Rise Dough (page 110), about the size of a volleyball

Unbleached bread flour

$\frac{1}{2}$ cup (125 mL) cornmeal (approx.)

2 cups (500 mL) hot water

EQUIPMENT

Baker's peel

Broiler pan

Baking stone

Plastic spray bottle of water

METHOD

1 Divide the dough into four portions. Place one portion on a floured surface and dust very lightly with flour. Flour your hands. Working the dough as little as possible and adding flour as necessary, form the dough into a 6-inch (15 cm) cylinder. Smooth the dough with your hands to form a soft, non-sticky skin. Pinch any seams together. Pinch each end into a point. Lightly flour any sticky places on the dough. The dough should feel soft and smooth all over, but not at all sticky. Repeat with the remaining dough.

2 Sprinkle the cornmeal on the baker's peel and place the rolls on the cornmeal, spacing them about 6 inches (15 cm) apart. Cover with plastic wrap and let rest at room temperature for 4 hours or until slightly risen.

3 About 30 minutes before baking, place the broiler pan on the lower shelf and the baking stone on the middle shelf of the oven. Preheat to 450°F (230°C).

4 Using a serrated knife, make three evenly spaced slashes, about 1 inch (2.5 cm) deep, across each roll, exposing the moist dough under the surface. With a dough scraper, gently scrape under each roll to make sure it isn't sticking to the peel. Add more cornmeal if necessary.

5 Carefully pull the middle rack of the oven out several inches. Hold the baker's peel level with the rack so that the first two rolls will slide sideways onto the hot stone. With a quick forward jerk of your arms, slide the first two rolls from the peel to the back of the stone. With another jerk, slide the second two rolls onto the front of the stone. Push the middle rack back in place. Pull the lower rack out, pour the hot water into the broiler pan and push the lower rack back in place. Spray the rolls with water. Close the oven door immediately so the steam will envelop the oven.

6 Bake for 12 to 14 minutes, spraying the rolls with water three times during baking, until the crust is a blistered medium golden brown and an instant-read thermometer inserted in the center of a roll registers at least 190°F (90°C). Remove the rolls to cool on a wire rack.

TIP

After baking, keep slow-rise breads wrapped in a brown paper bag, to keep their crust crisp and their crumb moist.

VARIATION

You can also use Slow-Rise Herbed Polenta Dough (page 112).

Coca Mallorquina

Makes 1 large flatbread, to serve 12

This Spanish "pizza," known as Coca Mallorquina, comes from Catalonia and Mallorca. Traditionally, this flatbread is baked in communal wood-burning ovens. A coca, or flatbread, can be a meal in itself, a snack or part of a tapas offering — great for entertaining. You can get the same wood-burning oven flavor using moistened fine wood chips in your indoor oven. If using the wood chips, be sure your kitchen is well ventilated.

INGREDIENTS

½ recipe prepared Easy Artisan Slow-Rise Dough (page 110), about the size of a volleyball

Unbleached bread flour

2 cups (500 mL) hot water

2 cloves garlic, minced

2 tsp (10 mL) coarse kosher or sea salt

6 tbsp (90 mL) extra virgin olive oil

2 tbsp (25 mL) freshly squeezed lemon juice

2 cups (500 mL) diced tomatoes

2 small zucchini, sliced paper-thin

¼ cup (50 mL) pine nuts

16 pitted oil-cured black olives

EQUIPMENT

Rolling pin

Large baking sheet, lined with parchment paper

Broiler pan

Baking stone

¼ cup (50 mL) fine dry hardwood chips, such as mesquite or apple, moistened with 2 tbsp (25 mL water (optional)

METHOD

1 Place dough on a floured surface and dust very lightly with flour. Flour your hands and the rolling pin. Working the dough as little as possible and adding flour as necessary, roll out the dough into a 12- by 10-inch (30 by 25 cm) rectangle. Lightly flour any sticky places on the dough. The dough should feel soft and smooth all over, but not at all sticky. Transfer to the prepared baking sheet.

2 In a small bowl, using a spoon or a fork, mash together garlic and salt. Stir in oil and lemon juice.

3 Brush half the garlic mixture over the dough. Arrange tomatoes and zucchini over the garlic mixture, leaving a 1-inch (2.5 cm) perimeter. Sprinkle with pine nuts and olives.

4 Cover with plastic wrap and let rest at room temperature for 2 hours or until slightly risen.

5 About 30 minutes before baking, place the broiler pan on the lower shelf and the baking stone on the middle shelf of the oven. Preheat to 450°F (230°C). For the wood-burning oven technique, place the moistened wood chips in a small metal pan next to the broiler pan on the lower shelf. They will start to smolder and release wisps of smoke.

6 Drizzle flatbread with remaining garlic mixture.

7 Carefully pull the middle rack of the oven out several inches. Place the baking sheet on the hot stone. Push the middle rack back in place. Pull the lower rack out, pour the hot water into the broiler pan and push the lower rack back in place. Close the oven door immediately so the steam will envelop the oven.

8 Bake for 20 to 22 minutes or until the crust is puffed and golden brown. Remove from pan and transfer to a wire rack to cool. Remove the smoldering wood chips from the oven, let cool completely, then discard.

TIP

Use a mandolin or a very sharp knife to slice the zucchini.

Coca Andalucia

Use 8 oz (250 g) thinly sliced serrano or Iberico ham and 8 oz (250 g) shaved Manchego cheese in place of the garlic mixture and vegetables. Drizzle with olive oil before baking.

Slow-Rise Ciabatta

Makes 1 large loaf, to serve 12 to 16

Ciabatta is also known as Italian slipper bread, as the shape of the bread resembles ballet shoes. Ciabatta uses both biga (or naturally leavened starter) and yeast starter, along with a touch of milk and olive oil, for a honeycombed crumb and a crisp, blistered crust. If you've made ciabatta before and beaten it with a stand mixer, you'll be surprised that you can make it this way. It's the same batter-like dough, but you have much less work — you just have to wait longer. But that's the magic of the no-knead, slow-rise method. You'll need to spray the top of the loaf as it bakes, to make the smooth crust attain its characteristic blister.

INGREDIENTS

2 cups (500 mL) unbleached bread flour

2½ tsp (12 mL) instant or bread machine yeast

2½ tsp (12 mL) fine kosher or sea salt

1½ cups (375 mL) filtered or bottled spring water, at room temperature

1 tbsp (15 mL) olive oil

1 tbsp (15 mL) milk

½ recipe prepared Biga (page 111)

½ cup (125 mL) cornmeal

2 cups (500 mL) hot water

EQUIPMENT

4-cup (1 L) bowl

Wooden spoon or Danish dough whisk

Baker's peel

Flexible cutting board, floured

Broiler pan

Baking stone

Plastic spray bottle of water

METHOD

1. Spoon the flour into a measuring cup, level with a knife or your finger, then dump the flour into a mixing bowl.

2. Add the yeast and salt to the flour. Stir together with a wooden spoon or Danish dough whisk. In a measuring cup, combine water, oil and milk. Add water mixture and biga to the flour mixture and stir together until just moistened. Beat 40 strokes, scraping the bottom and the sides of the bowl, until the dough forms a thick, spongy mass.

3. Cover the bowl with plastic wrap and let ferment at room temperature (72°F/22°C) in a draft-free place for 4 to 6 hours or until it almost reaches the top of the bowl.

4. Use that day or place the bowl, covered with plastic wrap, in the refrigerator for up to 3 days before baking.

5. Place dough on a floured surface and dust very lightly with flour. Flour your hands. Working the dough as little as possible and adding flour as necessary, scrape the dough up and over itself, flouring as you go, until the dough has settled into a 16-inch (40 cm) long oval and is not sticky. Scrape the dough up from the floured surface at intervals to make sure it isn't sticking to the surface. Add more flour when necessary. Smooth the dough with your hands to form a soft, non-sticky skin. Lightly flour any sticky places on the dough. The dough should feel soft all over, but not at all sticky.

6. Leaving the dough on the floured surface, cover with plastic wrap and let rest at room temperature for 1 hour or until slightly risen.

7. About 30 minutes before baking, place the broiler pan on the lower shelf and the baking stone on the middle shelf of the oven. Preheat to 450°F (230°C).

8. Remove the plastic wrap from the ciabatta and pinch any seams that remain. Spray with water. Sprinkle the cornmeal on the baker's peel. Using the cutting board, and adding flour to any sticky spots on the dough, transfer the ciabatta to the peel. Spray again with water.

9. Carefully pull the middle rack of the oven out several inches. Hold the baker's peel level with the rack so that the ciabatta will slide onto the center of the hot stone. With a quick forward jerk of your arms, slide the ciabatta from the peel to the stone. Push the middle rack back in place. Pull the lower rack out, pour the hot water into the broiler pan and push the lower rack back in place. Close the oven door immediately so the steam will envelop the oven.

10. Bake for 20 to 23 minutes, spraying the loaf with water three times during baking, until the crust is a blistered medium golden brown and an instant-read thermometer inserted in the center of the loaf registers at least 190°F (90°C). Remove the loaf to cool on a wire rack.

TIP

After baking, keep slow-rise and naturally leavened breads wrapped in a brown paper bag, to keep their crust crisp and their crumb moist.

BAKING WITH CANADIAN BREAD FLOUR

Canadian bread flour generally has a higher protein content than U.S. bread flour. That means it absorbs more water. If using Canadian bread flour, you may need to use slightly more water to avoid a dry dough. Begin by adding an extra tablespoon or two (15 to 30 mL) of water and continue adding until a soft dough is formed.

Easy Artisan Gluten-Free Dough

Makes enough dough for bread, rolls, pizza or flatbread to serve 12 to 16

For this dough, you need an assortment of gluten-free flours to get the approximate color, flavor and texture. Xanthan gum, which is made from corn and can be a little pricey, provides a framework or structure similar to that of gluten. You can find gluten-free flours and xanthan gum in the specialty baking section of the grocery or health food store, or online at www.bobsredmill.com. The eggs, vinegar, brown sugar and applesauce soften and round out the flavor of the dough.

For some people who are gluten-intolerant, even the tiniest speck of gluten can be a problem, so make sure that all ingredients you put in the dough are gluten-free. Read the labels of manufactured products to make sure nothing has been processed in a facility that also processes gluten. If you also make wheat-based doughs, run your bowls, measuring cups, dough whisk, etc., through the dishwasher again before making a gluten-free dough.

In addition, some people with gluten-intolerance are also allergic to dairy products and possibly eggs, so each recipe offers substitutes.

INGREDIENTS

2 cups (500 mL) stone-ground brown rice flour

2 cups (500 mL) tapioca flour or potato starch

2 cups (500 mL) chickpea (garbanzo bean) flour

1 cup (250 mL) cornstarch or corn flour

2 tbsp (25 mL) xanthan gum

2 tbsp (25 mL) instant or bread machine yeast

1 tbsp (15 mL) fine table or kosher salt

6 eggs, or equivalent substitute (see Allergy-Free Variation)

⅓ cup (75 mL) packed light or dark brown sugar

2 cups (500 mL) lukewarm water (about 100°F/38°C)

1 cup (250 mL) unsweetened applesauce

⅓ cup (75 mL) vegetable oil (preferably canola)

2 tsp (10 mL) cider vinegar

EQUIPMENT

Instant-read thermometer

16-cup (4 L) mixing bowl

Wire whisk or Danish dough whisk

METHOD

1 One at a time, spoon the rice flour, tapioca flour, chickpea flour and cornstarch into a measuring cup, level with a knife or your finger, then dump into the mixing bowl. Combine well.

2 Add the xanthan gum, yeast and salt to the flour mixture. Stir together with a wire whisk or Danish dough whisk. In a large bowl, lightly beat eggs. Whisk in brown sugar, water, applesauce, oil and vinegar until well combined. Pour into the flour mixture and whisk until a smooth, very loose, batter-like dough forms.

3 Cover the bowl with plastic wrap and let rise at room temperature (72°F/22°C) in a draft-free place for 2 hours or until the dough has risen nearly to the top of the bowl and has a thick, golden, mashed potato–like appearance.

4 Use that day or place the dough, covered with plastic wrap, in the refrigerator for up to 3 days before baking.

CAUTION

Just be aware that this is a unique dough — at first, it resembles a very wet batter. After an hour, it thickens to the consistency of brownie batter. After 2 hours, it rises to about 1 inch (2.5 cm) from the top of the bowl and looks like cornbread batter or golden mashed potatoes. The raw dough doesn't taste like a yeast bread dough. But, magically, during baking, it makes a gluten-free white whole-grain bread with a moist and tender crumb, browned crust and mellow, yeasty flavor.

TIPS

- Combining 1 cup (250 mL) hot with 1 cup (250 mL) cold tap water will result in lukewarm water of approximately 100°F (38°C).
- Before storing the dough in the refrigerator, use a permanent marker to write the date on the plastic wrap, so you'll know when you made your dough — and when to use it up 3 days later.

ALLERGY-FREE VARIATION

- People who are gluten-intolerant are often allergic to eggs and dairy as well. This recipe is already gluten- and dairy-free; for egg-free, use the equivalent amount of liquid egg substitute for 6 eggs in place of the eggs.

Gluten-Free Soy Dough

Replace half or all of the chickpea flour with soy flour.

Gluten-Free Cornmeal Pepper Dough

Makes enough dough for bread, rolls, pizza or flatbread to serve 12 to 16

You can get wonderful savory flavor in a gluten-free bread with this dough.

INGREDIENTS

2 cups (500 mL) stone-ground brown rice flour

2 cups (500 mL) tapioca flour or potato starch

2 cups (500 mL) plain yellow cornmeal

1 cup (250 mL) cornstarch or corn flour

2 tbsp (25 mL) xanthan gum

2 tbsp (25 mL) instant or bread machine yeast

1 tbsp (15 mL) fine table or kosher salt

1 tbsp (15 mL) freshly ground white pepper

1 tbsp (15 mL) freshly ground black pepper

1 tbsp (15 mL) granualted sugar

6 eggs, or equivalent substitute (see Allergy-Free Variation)

1/3 cup (75 mL) packed light or dark brown sugar

2 cups (500 mL) lukewarm water (about 100°F/38°C)

1 cup (250 mL) canned pumpkin purée (not pumpkin pie mix)

1/3 cup (75 mL) vegetable oil (preferably canola)

2 tsp (10 mL) cider vinegar

EQUIPMENT

Instant-read thermometer

16-cup (4 L) mixing bowl

Wire whisk or Danish dough whisk

METHOD

1 One at a time, spoon the rice flour, tapioca flour, cornmeal and cornstarch into a measuring cup, level with a knife or your finger, then dump into the mixing bowl. Combine well.

2 Add the xanthan gum, yeast, salt, white pepper, black pepper and sugar to the flour mixture. Stir together with a wire whisk or Danish dough whisk. In a large bowl, lightly beat eggs. Whisk in brown sugar, water, pumpkin purée, oil and vinegar until well combined. Pour into the flour mixture and whisk until a smooth, very loose, batter-like dough forms.

3 Cover the bowl with plastic wrap and let rise at room temperature (72°F/22°C) in a draft-free place for 2 hours or until the dough has risen nearly to the top of the bowl and has a thick, golden, mashed potato–like appearance.

4 Use that day or place the dough, covered with plastic wrap, in the refrigerator for up to 3 days before baking.

ALLERGY-FREE VARIATION

People who are gluten-intolerant are often allergic to eggs and dairy as well. This recipe is already gluten- and dairy-free; for egg-free, use the equivalent amount of liquid egg substitute for 6 eggs in place of the eggs.

Mill
Notre ligne de produits
est variée et vaste. Pour
l'informations et des recettes,
veuillez visiter notre site web
www.bobsredmill.com
HANE
K

Gluten-Free Caraway "Rye" Dough

Makes enough dough for bread, rolls, pizza or flatbread to serve 12 to 16

Caraway, molasses and cocoa powder give the taste of rye without the rye flour.

INGREDIENTS

2 cups (500 mL) stone-ground brown rice flour

2 cups (500 mL) tapioca flour or potato starch

2 cups (500 mL) chickpea (garbanzo bean) flour

1 cup (250 mL) cornstarch or corn flour

2 tbsp (25 mL) xanthan gum

2 tbsp (25 mL) instant or bread machine yeast

2 tbsp (25 mL) caraway seeds

1 tbsp (15 mL) fine table or kosher salt

6 eggs, or equivalent substitute (see Allergy-Free Variation)

½ cup (125 mL) unsweetened cocoa powder

2 cups (500 mL) lukewarm water (about 100°F/38°C)

6 tbsp (90 mL) light (fancy) molasses

⅓ cup (75 mL) vegetable oil (preferably canola)

2 tsp (10 mL) cider vinegar

EQUIPMENT

Instant-read thermometer

16-cup (4 L) mixing bowl

Wire whisk or Danish dough whisk

METHOD

1. One at a time, spoon the rice flour, tapioca flour, chickpea flour and cornstarch into a measuring cup, level with a knife or your finger, then dump into the mixing bowl. Combine well.

2. Add the xanthan gum, yeast, caraway seeds and salt to the flour mixture. Stir together with a wire whisk or Danish dough whisk. In a large bowl, lightly beat eggs. Whisk in cocoa, water, molasses, oil and vinegar until well combined. Pour into the flour mixture and whisk until a smooth, very loose, batter-like dough forms.

3. Cover the bowl with plastic wrap and let rise at room temperature (72°F/22°C) in a draft-free place for 2 hours or until the dough has risen nearly to the top of the bowl and has a thick, golden, mashed potato–like appearance.

4. Use that day or place the dough, covered with plastic wrap, in the refrigerator for up to 3 days before baking.

ALLERGY-FREE VARIATION

People who are gluten-intolerant are often allergic to eggs and dairy as well. This recipe is already gluten- and dairy-free; for egg-free, use the equivalent amount of liquid egg substitute for 6 eggs in place of the eggs.

Gluten-Free Bread

Makes 2 loaves, to serve 16

This moist loaf, with a tender crumb and mellow, yeasty flavor, satisfies the need for "white" bread. Use it for breakfast toast or sandwiches. It can be wrapped and stored in the refrigerator for up to 3 days.

INGREDIENTS

1 recipe prepared Easy Artisan Gluten-Free Dough (page 124)

2 cups (500 mL) hot water

EQUIPMENT

Two 9- by 5-inch (23 by 12.5 cm) loaf pans, greased

Broiler pan

Baking stone

METHOD

1 Cut dough in half and place each half in a prepared loaf pan. Even out the batter-like dough and smooth the top with a dough scraper or spatula.

2 Cover with tea towels and let rest at room temperature for 40 minutes.

3 About 30 minutes before baking, place the broiler pan on the lower shelf and the baking stone on the middle shelf of the oven. Preheat to 350°F (180°C).

4 Carefully pull the middle rack of the oven out several inches. Place the loaf pans at least 3 inches (7.5 cm) apart on the hot stone. Push the middle rack back in place. Pull the lower rack out, pour the hot water into the broiler pan and push the lower rack back in place. Close the oven door immediately so the steam will envelop the oven.

5 Bake for 27 to 30 minutes or until the crust is a medium dark brown and an instant-read thermometer inserted in the center of the loaves registers at least 190°F (90°C). Transfer to a wire rack to cool in pans for 10 minutes. Remove from pans and let cool on rack.

VARIATION

Gluten-Free Soy Dough (variation, page 125), Gluten-Free Cornmeal Pepper Dough (page 126) or Gluten-Free Caraway "Rye" Dough (page 128).

Seeded Gluten-Free Bread

Before baking, brush the top of each loaf with beaten egg white or an equivalent substitute and press on poppy, fennel, millet, toasted pumpkin or sunflower seeds, or a combination.

Gluten-Free Pizza

Makes 1 pizza, to serve 8 to 12

People who are intolerant to the gluten in wheat still want to eat what everybody else does. And who can blame them? As long as the pizza toppings are also gluten-free (check the labels), there's no reason why those who are gluten-intolerant can't enjoy pizza. If dairy is a concern, use soy cheese or equivalents. This recipe makes a rectangular pizza (it's easy to spread the batter-like dough into this shape)

INGREDIENTS

½ recipe prepared Easy Artisan Gluten-Free Dough (page 124)

1 cup (250 mL) gluten-free pizza sauce

2 cups (500 mL) thinly sliced mushrooms

2 cups (500 mL) sliced pepperoni, cooked gluten-free Italian sausage or ham

2 cups (500 mL) shredded mozzarella, provolone or dairy-free cheese product

Olive oil

2 cups (500 mL) hot water

EQUIPMENT

Large baking sheet, lined with parchment paper

Broiler pan

Baking stone

METHOD

1 Place dough on the prepared baking sheet. Using a water-moistened plastic spatula or your hands, spread the dough into a 14- by 10-inch (35 by 25 cm) rectangle.

2 Cover with a tea towel and let rest at room temperature for 40 minutes.

3 About 30 minutes before baking, place the broiler pan on the lower shelf and the baking stone on the middle shelf of the oven. Preheat to 350°F (180°C).

4 Spread pizza sauce over the dough. Arrange mushrooms and pepperoni over the sauce, then sprinkle with cheese. Drizzle with olive oil.

5 Carefully pull the middle rack of the oven out several inches. Place the baking sheet on the hot stone. Push the middle rack back in place. Pull the lower rack out, pour the hot water into the broiler pan and push the lower rack back in place. Close the oven door immediately so the steam will envelop the oven.

6 Bake for 25 to 30 minutes or until the crust is lightly browned and the toppings are bubbling. Slice and serve.

Gluten-Free Sandwich Buns

Makes 12 buns

When you want a gluten-free bun for your sizzling burger, this is it. Make this large batch and freeze extras for up to 3 months. Because the dough is so batter-like, use 4-inch (10 cm) mini pie pans (available at kitchen shops) to form the buns.

INGREDIENTS

2 cups (500 mL) stone-ground brown rice flour

2 cups (500 mL) tapioca flour or potato starch

4 tsp (20 mL) xanthan gum

1/4 cup (50 mL) granulated sugar

2 tbsp (25 mL) instant or bread machine yeast

2 tsp (10 mL) fine table or kosher salt

3 eggs, or equivalent substitute (see Allergy-Free Variation)

1 1/2 cups (375 mL) lukewarm milk or plant-based milk (about 100°F/38°C)

1/2 cup (125 mL) lukewarm water (about 100°F/38°C)

1/4 cup (50 mL) vegetable oil (preferably canola)

1 tsp (5 mL) cider vinegar

1 egg white, beaten, or equivalent substitute

Poppy or sesame seeds

EQUIPMENT

Instant-read thermometer

16-cup (4 L) mixing bowl

Wire whisk or Danish dough whisk

Twelve 4-inch (10 cm) mini pie pans, brushed with vegetable oil

Baking stone

METHOD

1 One at a time, spoon the rice flour and tapioca flour into a measuring cup, level with a knife or your finger, then dump into the mixing bowl. Combine well.

2 Add the xanthan gum, sugar, yeast and salt to the flour mixture. Stir together with a wire whisk or Danish dough whisk. In a large bowl, lightly beat eggs. Whisk in milk, water, oil and vinegar until well combined. Pour into the flour mixture and whisk until a smooth, very loose, batter-like dough forms.

3 Cover the bowl with plastic wrap and let rise at room temperature (72°F/22°C) in a draft-free place for 2 hours or until the dough has risen nearly to the top of the bowl and has a thick, mashed potato–like appearance.

4 Use that day or place the dough, covered with plastic wrap, in the refrigerator for up to 3 days before baking.

5 Spoon the dough into the prepared pans, dividing evenly.

6 Cover with tea towels and let rest at room temperature for 40 minutes.

7 About 30 minutes before baking, place the baking stone on the middle shelf of the oven. Preheat to 350°F (180°C).

8 Brush the top of the dough with beaten egg white and sprinkle with poppy seeds.

9 Carefully pull the middle rack of the oven out several inches. Place six of the pie pans on the hot stone. Push the middle rack back in place.

10 Bake for 15 to 20 minutes or until an instant-read thermometer inserted in the center of a bun registers at least 190°F (90°C). Transfer to a wire rack to cool. Repeat with the remaining pans.

TIP

Before storing the dough in the refrigerator, use a permanent marker to write the date on the plastic wrap, so you'll know when you made your dough — and when to use it up 3 days later.

ALLERGY-FREE VARIATION

To make this recipe dairy- and egg-free, use a plant-based milk in place of cow's milk and liquid egg substitute in place of eggs and egg white.

Gluten-Free Cinnamon Rolls

Makes 12 rolls

With a looser dough, these rolls are a little trickier to make than those made with a wheat dough, but they're well worth the effort. Sometimes, only the comfort of a cinnamon roll will do.

INGREDIENTS

$\frac{1}{2}$ recipe prepared Easy Artisan Gluten-Free Dough (page 124)

1 recipe Cinnamon Filling (page 208)

2 cups (500 mL) hot water

Easy Artisan Glaze (page 212)

EQUIPMENT

Flexible cutting board, lightly sprayed with water

Two 20-inch (50 cm) long pieces of waxed or parchment paper

Two 6-cup muffin tins, greased

Broiler pan

Baking stone

METHOD

1 Divide the dough in half. Spray the waxed paper with nonstick spray and place, sprayed side up, on a flat surface, one paper next to the other. Transfer one dough portion to a prepared paper. Using a water-moistened plastic spatula or your hands, spread the dough into a 14- by 10-inch (35 by 25 cm) rectangle. Spread with half the Cinnamon Filling. Starting with a long end, gently lift up the paper and nudge or scrape the dough so it rolls over on itself. Keep nudging and rolling until you have a cylinder. With a dough scraper, gently cut the cylinder into six $1\frac{1}{2}$-inch (4 cm) pieces. Repeat the process with the remaining dough, paper and filling.

2 Place each piece, cut side up, in a prepared muffin cup. Cover with tea towels and let rest at room temperature for 40 minutes.

3 About 30 minutes before baking, place the broiler pan on the lower shelf and the baking stone on the middle shelf of the oven. Preheat to 350°F (180°C).

4 Carefully pull the middle rack of the oven out several inches. Place the muffin tins on the hot stone. Push the middle rack back in place. Pull the lower rack out, pour the hot water into the broiler pan and push the lower rack back in place. Close the oven door immediately so the steam will envelop the oven.

5 Bake for 15 to 18 minutes or until risen and lightly browned. Transfer to a wire rack to cool. Once cool, drizzle with glaze.

ALLERGY-FREE VARIATION

If dairy is a concern, make the Cinnamon Filling with dairy-free margarine and the Easy Artisan Glaze with a plant-based milk. Make sure the vanilla you use in the glaze is labeled "gluten-free." Even the tiniest speck of gluten from a manufacturing plant that processes many different foods can prompt a reaction.

Easy Artisan Sweet Dough

Makes enough dough for festive breads, coffee cakes, tea rings or sweet rolls to serve 12 to 16

Substituting milk for the water and adding sugar, melted butter and eggs to Easy Artisan Dough transforms it into a sweet dough. With these additions, the dough is heavier, and thus needs more yeast — and stronger unbleached bread flour — to make it rise and achieve the appropriate crumb. Sweet dough recipes do best when baked on a baking sheet lined with parchment paper (sweet fillings can ooze out of the dough and blacken on your baking stone), and at a lower temperature: 400°F (200°C). With this master dough, you can produce wonderful coffee cakes, festive breads and sweet rolls with a moist, feathery crumb. The dough will last for only 3 days in the refrigerator before it turns bitter.

INGREDIENTS

6½ cups (1.625 L) unbleached bread flour

2 tbsp (25 mL) instant or bread machine yeast

1½ tbsp (22 mL) fine kosher salt

2½ cups (625 mL) lukewarm milk (about 100°F/38°C)

1 cup (250 mL) granulated sugar

½ cup (125 mL) unsalted butter, melted

2 eggs

EQUIPMENT

Instant-read thermometer

16-cup (4 L) mixing bowl

4-cup (1 L) glass measuring cup

Wooden spoon or Danish dough whisk

METHOD

1 Spoon the flour into a measuring cup, level with a knife or your finger, then dump the flour into the mixing bowl.

2 Add the yeast and salt to the flour. Stir together with a wooden spoon or Danish dough whisk. In the glass measuring cup, combine milk, sugar and butter. Using a fork, beat in eggs. Pour into the flour mixture and stir together until just moistened. Beat 40 strokes, scraping the bottom and the sides of the bowl, until the dough forms a lumpy, sticky mass.

3 Cover the bowl with plastic wrap and let rise at room temperature (72°F/22°C) in a draft-free place for 2 hours or until the dough has risen to about 2 inches (5 cm) under the rim of the bowl and has a sponge-like appearance.

4 Use that day or place the dough, covered with plastic wrap, in the refrigerator for up to 3 days before baking.

TIPS

- Microwaving cold milk for about 2 minutes on High will result in lukewarm milk of approximately 100°F (38°C).
- Before storing the dough in the refrigerator, use a permanent marker to write the date on the plastic wrap, so you'll know when you made your dough — and when to use it up 3 days later.

Sweet Citrus-Scented Dough

Add 2 tsp (10 mL) freshly grated lemon or orange zest to the flour in Step 1.

BAKING WITH CANADIAN BREAD FLOUR

Canadian bread flour generally has a higher protein content than U.S. bread flour. That means it absorbs more water. If using Canadian bread flour, you may need to use slightly more water to avoid a dry dough. Begin by adding an extra tablespoon or two (15 to 30 mL) of water and continue adding until a soft dough is formed.

EASY ARTISAN SWEET BREADS IN MINUTES A DAY

Day 1: Stir the dough together and let rise. Bake, or cover and chill.

Days 2–3: Remove part of the dough, form and bake.

NUT	HOW USED
Almonds	Ground for filling, sliced for decoration, almond extract for flavoring glazes
Hazelnuts	Ground for filling
Peanuts	Peanut butter for filling
Pecans	Ground for filling, whole halves for decoration
Pistachios	Ground for filling, roasted and shelled for decoration
Walnuts	Ground or roasted and chopped for filling

To toast whole nuts or halves, spread them on a baking sheet and toast in a 350°F (180°C) oven for 10 to 15 minutes or until golden brown.

Swedish Tea Ring Dough

Makes enough dough for tea rings or sweet rolls to serve 12 to 16

A hint of cardamom scents this dough, the pride of Swedish bakers.

INGREDIENTS

6½ cups (1.625 L) unbleached bread flour

2 tbsp (25 mL) instant or bread machine yeast

1½ tbsp (22 mL) fine kosher salt

2 tsp (10 mL) ground cardamom

2½ cups (625 mL) lukewarm milk (about 100°F/38°C)

1 cup (250 mL) granulated sugar

½ cup (125 mL) unsalted butter, melted

2 eggs

EQUIPMENT

Instant-read thermometer

16-cup (4 L) mixing bowl

4-cup (1 L) glass measuring cup

Wooden spoon or Danish dough whisk

METHOD

1 Spoon the flour into a measuring cup, level with a knife or your finger, then dump the flour into the mixing bowl.

2 Add the yeast, salt and cardamom to the flour. Stir together with a wooden spoon or Danish dough whisk. In the glass measuring cup, combine milk, sugar and butter. Using a fork, beat in eggs. Pour into the flour mixture and stir together until just moistened. Beat 40 strokes, scraping the bottom and the sides of the bowl, until the dough forms a lumpy, sticky mass.

3 Cover the bowl with plastic wrap and let rise at room temperature (72°F/22°C) in a draft-free place for 2 hours or until the dough has risen to about 2 inches (5 cm) under the rim of the bowl and has a sponge-like appearance.

4 Use that day or place the dough, covered with plastic wrap, in the refrigerator for up to 3 days before baking.

TIP

Instead of the ground cardamom, you can purchase 24 cardamom pods and crush the seeds.

BAKING WITH CANADIAN BREAD FLOUR

Canadian bread flour generally has a higher protein content than U.S. bread flour. That means it absorbs more water. If using Canadian bread flour, you may need to use slightly more water to avoid a dry dough. Begin by adding an extra tablespoon or two (15 to 30 mL) of water and continue adding until a soft dough is formed.

Cardamom and Cinnamon-Scented Swedish Tea Ring

Makes 1 large tea ring, to serve 12 to 16

INGREDIENTS

½ recipe prepared Swedish Tea Ring Dough (page 138), about the size of a volleyball

Unbleached bread flour

½ recipe Cinnamon Filling (page 208)

2 cups (500 mL) hot water

Almond Glaze (variation, page 213)

1 cup (250 mL) green candied cherries (optional)

1 cup red candied cherries (optional)

EQUIPMENT

Rolling pin

Flexible cutting board,

floured, or two metal

spatulas

Baking sheet, lined with

parchment paper

Broiler pan

Baking stone

METHOD

1 Place dough on a floured surface and dust very lightly with flour. Flour your hands and the rolling pin. Working the dough as little as possible and adding flour as necessary, roll out the dough into an 18- by 12-inch (45 by 30 cm) rectangle. Spread cinnamon filling over the dough, leaving a 1-inch (2.5 cm) perimeter. Starting with a long end, roll up the dough into a cylinder. If the dough begins to stick to the surface, use a dough scraper to push flour under the dough and scrape it up. Gently press and squeeze as you're rolling, to form the dough into a solid cylinder. Pinch the long seam closed. Bring the ends together to form a circle and pinch closed. Lightly flour any sticky places on the dough. The dough should feel soft and smooth all over, but not at all sticky.

2 Using the cutting board or two metal spatulas, transfer the tea ring to the prepared baking sheet, seam side down. With kitchen shears, starting from the outer rim, cut diagonal slashes in the tea ring, three-quarters of the way through the dough, at 2-inch (5 cm) intervals all around the ring. Gently fan the slices, going in the same direction, so the filling shows. Cover with a tea towel and let rest at room temperature for 40 minutes.

3 About 30 minutes before baking, place the broiler pan on the lower shelf and the baking stone on the middle shelf of the oven. Preheat to 400°F (200°C).

4 Carefully pull the middle rack of the oven out several inches. Place the baking sheet on the hot stone. Push the middle rack back in place. Pull the lower rack out, pour the hot water into the broiler pan and push the lower rack back in place. Close the oven door immediately so the steam will envelop the oven.

5 Bake for 20 to 22 minutes or until risen and browned and an instant-read thermometer inserted in the center of the loaf registers at least 190°F (90°C). Remove from pan and transfer to a wire rack to cool. Once cool, drizzle with glaze. Garnish with green and red candied cherries, if desired.

VARIATION

Try with Easy Artisan Dough (page 36) or Easy Artisan Whole-Grain Dough (page 54), made with white whole wheat flour.

Chocolate Hazelnut Swirl Loaf

Makes 1 loaf, to serve 12

This is a rich, decadent bread. For the best flavor, use the best dark chocolate. If you really want to gild the lily, drizzle the loaf with both Easy Artisan Glaze (page 212) and Chocolate Glaze (page 209).

INGREDIENTS

½ recipe prepared Easy Artisan Sweet Dough (page 136), about the size of a volleyball

Unbleached bread flour

½ cup (125 mL) Toasted Hazelnut Filling (variation, page 204)

½ cup (125 mL) finely chopped dark chocolate or chocolate chips

2 cups (500 mL) hot water

Easy Artisan Glaze (page 212)

EQUIPMENT

Rolling pin (optional)

Flexible cutting board, floured, or two metal spatulas

Baking sheet, lined with parchment paper

Broiler pan

Baking stone

METHOD

1 Place dough on a floured surface and dust very lightly with flour. Flour your hands and the rolling pin, if using. Working the dough as little as possible and adding flour as necessary, pat or roll out the dough into a 10- by 9-inch (25 by 23 cm) rectangle. Spread hazelnut filling over the dough, leaving a 1-inch (2.5 cm) perimeter. Sprinkle chocolate over the filling. Starting with a long end, roll up the dough into a cylinder. If the dough begins to stick to the surface, use a dough scraper to push flour under the dough and scrape it up. Gently press and squeeze as you're rolling, to form the dough into a solid cylinder. Pinch the ends and long seam closed. Lightly flour any sticky places on the dough. The dough should feel soft and smooth all over, but not at all sticky.

2 Using the cutting board or two metal spatulas, transfer the loaf to the prepared baking sheet, seam side down. Cover with a tea towel and let rest at room temperature for 40 minutes.

3 About 30 minutes before baking, place the broiler pan on the lower shelf and the baking stone on the middle shelf of the oven. Preheat to 400°F (200°C).

4 Carefully pull the middle rack of the oven out several inches. Place the baking sheet on the hot stone. Push the middle rack back in place. Pull the lower rack out, pour the hot water into the broiler pan and push the lower rack back in place. Close the oven door immediately so the steam will envelop the oven.

5 Bake for 27 to 30 minutes or until the crust is dark brown and an instant-read thermometer inserted in the center of the loaf registers at least 190°F (90°C). Remove from pan and transfer to a wire rack to cool. Once cool, drizzle with glaze.

TIP

You can use prepared chocolate hazelnut spread in place of the hazelnut filling.

VARIATION

You can also use Easy Artisan Dough (page 36) or Easy Artisan Whole-Grain Dough (page 54), made with white whole wheat flour.

Chocolate Peanut Butter Swirl Loaf

Substitute $\frac{1}{2}$ cup (125 mL) peanut butter for the hazelnut filling.

Raspberry Almond Swirl Loaf

Substitute $\frac{1}{2}$ cup (125 mL) Danish Almond Filling (page 204) or prepared almond paste for the hazelnut filling and $\frac{1}{2}$ cup (125 mL) good-quality seedless raspberry preserves for the chocolate. Spread the preserves over the almond filling in step 1, then proceed with the recipe.

Classic Cinnamon Rolls

Makes 8 rolls

Cinnamon rolls are true comfort food. Just the scent of them baking makes you feel good.

INGREDIENTS

½ recipe prepared Easy Artisan Sweet Dough (page 136), about the size of a volleyball

Unbleached bread flour

½ recipe Cinnamon Filling (page 208)

2 cups (500 mL) hot water

Easy Artisan Glaze (page 212)

EQUIPMENT

Rolling pin

8-inch (20 cm) round cake pan, buttered

Broiler pan

Baking stone

METHOD

1 Place dough on a floured surface and dust very lightly with flour. Flour your hands and the rolling pin. Working the dough as little as possible and adding flour as necessary, roll out the dough into a 12- by 8-inch (30 by 20 cm) rectangle. Spread cinnamon filling over the dough, leaving a ½-inch (1 cm) perimeter. Starting with a short end, roll up the dough into a cylinder. If the dough begins to stick to the surface, use a dough scraper to push flour under the dough and scrape it up. Gently press and squeeze as you're rolling to form the dough into a solid cylinder. With a pastry brush, brush off any excess flour. Pinch the long seam closed, then turn seam side down. With the dough scraper, slice the cylinder into 1-inch (2.5 cm) pieces.

2 Place the rolls, cut side up, in the prepared pan so that they are almost touching. Cover with a tea towel and let rest at room temperature for 40 minutes.

3 About 30 minutes before baking, place the broiler pan on the lower shelf and the baking stone on the middle shelf of the oven. Preheat to 400°F (200°C).

4 Carefully pull the middle rack of the oven out several inches. Place the cake pan on the hot stone. Push the middle rack back in place. Pull the lower rack out, pour the hot water into the broiler pan and push the lower rack back in place. Close the oven door immediately so the steam will envelop the oven.

5 Bake for 30 to 34 minutes or until an instant-read thermometer inserted in the center of the rolls registers at least 190°F (90°C). Transfer to a wire rack to cool in pan. Once cool, drizzle with glaze.

VARIATION

You can also use Swedish Tea Ring Dough (page 138), Easy Artisan Dough (page 36) or Easy Artisan Whole-Grain Dough (page 54), made with white whole wheat flour.

Pecan Sticky Buns

In a saucepan, melt $\frac{1}{2}$ cup (125 mL) unsalted butter over medium heat. Add $\frac{1}{2}$ cup (125 mL) packed light or dark brown sugar and stir until the mixture bubbles and thickens. Pour into the prepared cake pan and set aside to cool while you form the rolls. Scatter $\frac{2}{3}$ cup (150 mL) chopped toasted pecans over the bottom of the pan. Place the rolls, cut side up, in the prepared pan and proceed with the recipe. After baking, let cool in pan briefly, then invert the rolls onto a serving plate and serve sticky side up. Omit the glaze.

Cider-Glazed Cinnamon Apple Rolls

Makes 8 rolls

This recipe takes the classic cinnamon roll one step further with the tart crunch of apple and a cider-spiked glaze.

INGREDIENTS

½ cup (125 mL) packed light or dark brown sugar

1 tbsp (15 mL) ground cinnamon

½ recipe prepared Easy Artisan Sweet Dough (page 136), about the size of a volleyball

Unbleached bread flour

½ cup (125 mL) finely chopped apple

2 cups (500 mL) hot water

Cider Glaze (variation, page 213)

EQUIPMENT

Rolling pin

8-inch (20 cm) round cake pan, buttered

Broiler pan

Baking stone

METHOD

1 In a small bowl, combine brown sugar and cinnamon.

2 Place dough on a floured surface and dust very lightly with flour. Flour your hands and the rolling pin. Working the dough as little as possible and adding flour as necessary, roll out the dough into a 12- by 8-inch (30 by 20 cm) rectangle. Sprinkle brown sugar mixture over the dough, leaving a ½-inch (1 cm) perimeter. Scatter apple over the filling. Starting with a short end, roll up the dough into a cylinder. If the dough begins to stick to the surface, use a dough scraper to push flour under the dough and scrape it up. Gently press and squeeze as you're rolling to form the dough into a solid cylinder. With a pastry brush, brush off any excess flour. Pinch the ends and long seam closed, then turn seam side down. With the dough scraper, slice the cylinder into 1-inch (2.5 cm) pieces.

3 Place the rolls, cut side up, in the prepared pan so that they are almost touching. Cover with a tea towel and let rest at room temperature for 40 minutes.

4 About 30 minutes before baking, place the broiler pan on the lower shelf and the baking stone on the middle shelf of the oven. Preheat to 400°F (200°C).

5 Carefully pull the middle rack of the oven out several inches. Place the cake pan on the hot stone. Push the middle rack back in place. Pull the lower rack out, pour the hot water into the broiler pan and push the lower rack back in place. Close the oven door immediately so the steam will envelop the oven.

6 Bake for 30 to 34 minutes or until an instant-read thermometer inserted in the center of the rolls registers at least 190°F (90°C). Transfer to a wire rack to cool in pan. Once cool, drizzle with glaze.

VARIATION

You can also use Swedish Tea Ring Dough (page 138), Easy Artisan Dough (page 36) or Easy Artisan Whole-Grain Dough (page 54), made with white whole wheat flour.

Apple Custard Kuchen

Makes 2 coffee cakes, to serve 12 to 16

The cinnamon-spiced apple custard, paired with a sweet yeast dough, will have everyone wanting second and third pieces. Good thing this recipe makes two coffee cakes!

INGREDIENTS

½ recipe prepared Easy Artisan Sweet Dough (page 136), about the size of a volleyball

Unbleached bread flour

½ cup (125 mL) granulated sugar

1 egg, beaten

1 cup (250 mL) heavy or whipping (35%) cream

1 cup (250 mL) Honey Spice Applesauce (page 200) or other chunky homemade applesauce

EQUIPMENT

Rolling pin

Two 8-inch (20 cm) square baking pans, buttered

Broiler pan

Baking stone

METHOD

1 Divide the dough in half. Transfer one half to a floured surface and dust very lightly with flour. Flour your hands and the rolling pin. Working the dough as little as possible and adding flour as necessary, roll out into a 10-inch (25 cm) square. Drape the dough over the rolling pin and transfer to one of the baking pans, fitting the dough into the bottom and up the sides. Repeat with the remaining dough.

2 Cover with tea towels and let rest at room temperature for 40 minutes.

3 About 30 minutes before baking, place the broiler pan on the lower shelf and the baking stone on the middle shelf of the oven. Preheat to 400°F (200°C).

4 Five minutes before baking, in a bowl, combine sugar, egg, cream and applesauce. Pour half the filling into each pan.

5 Carefully pull the middle rack of the oven out several inches. Place the baking pans on the hot stone. Push the middle rack back in place. Pull the lower rack out, pour the hot water into the broiler pan and push the lower rack back in place. Close the oven door immediately so the steam will envelop the oven.

6 Bake for 17 to 20 minutes or until filling has browned and crust is a medium reddish-brown. Transfer to a wire rack to cool in pans.

Apricot Kolache

Makes 24 rolls

From Old World Bohemia, kolache are small, sweet, yeast-risen cakes filled with preserves and drizzled with glaze. They're a classic offering for a morning coffee break with neighbors or at Czech heritage festivals.

INGREDIENTS

$\frac{1}{2}$ recipe prepared Easy Artisan Sweet Dough (page 136), about the size of a volleyball

Unbleached bread flour

$\frac{1}{2}$ cup (125 mL) good-quality apricot preserves

2 cups (500 mL) hot water

Almond Glaze (variation, page 213)

Clear or white sanding sugar

EQUIPMENT

2 large baking sheets, lined with parchment paper

Broiler pan

Baking stone

METHOD

1 Divide the dough in half. Transfer one half to a floured surface and dust very lightly with flour. Flour your hands. Working the dough as little as possible and adding flour as necessary, form the dough into a 12-inch (30 cm) cylinder. With a dough scraper, slice the cylinder into 1-inch (2.5 cm) pieces. Roll each piece into a ball. Lightly flour any sticky places on the dough. The dough should feel soft and smooth all over, but not at all sticky. Repeat with the remaining dough.

2 Place the rolls about 2 inches (5 cm) apart on the prepared baking sheets. Cover with a tea towel and let rest for 45 minutes.

3 About 30 minutes before baking, place the broiler pan on the lower shelf and the baking stone on the middle shelf of the oven. Preheat to 400°F (200°C).

4 With your knuckle or the handle of a wooden spoon, make an indentation in the center of each roll. Spoon 1 tsp (5 mL) preserves into each indentation.

5 Carefully pull the middle rack of the oven out several inches. Place one of the baking sheets on the hot stone. Push the middle rack back in place. Pull the lower rack out, pour the hot water into the broiler pan and push the lower rack back in place. Close the oven door immediately so the steam will envelop the oven.

6 Bake for 8 to 10 minutes or until the rolls are puffed and lightly browned. Remove from pan and transfer to a wire rack set over a baking sheet to cool. Repeat the baking process with the remaining rolls. Once cool, drizzle with glaze. Dust with sanding sugar.

TIP

Sanding sugar is available at baking supply shops or online.

Poppy Seed Kolache

Substitute $\frac{1}{2}$ cup (125 mL) Poppy Seed Filling (page 203) or prepared poppy seed filling for the apricot preserves and Lemon Glaze (variation, page 213) for the Almond Glaze.

Plum Kolache

Substitute $\frac{1}{2}$ cup (125 mL) good-quality plum preserves for the apricot preserves.

Easy Artisan Brioche Dough

Makes enough dough for bread, rolls, savarins or beignets to serve 12 to 16

Brioche is a sweet dough enriched with even more butter and eggs than sweet dough. With a slight tang of buttermilk to counter the richness, this dough makes fabulous festive breads, feathery rolls and wonderful beignets. With this easy recipe, Marie Antoinette's infamous retort, "Let them eat brioche," becomes a much more democratic possibility. No longer an exclusive specialty of French bakeries, rich and golden brioche can be made in your own kitchen. With brioche, you'll work with half the dough at a time. Brush traditional brioche shapes with an egg wash before baking. You won't need the egg wash for breads, rolls, beignets or savarins that are to be glazed or dusted with sugar.

INGREDIENTS

6½ cups (1.625 L) unbleached bread flour or a mixture of bread and all-purpose flour

½ cup (125 mL) granulated sugar

2 tbsp (25 mL) instant or bread machine yeast

1½ tbsp (22 mL) fine kosher salt

1 cup (250 mL) unsalted butter, melted

½ cup (125 mL) buttermilk

8 eggs, beaten

¾ cup (175 mL) lukewarm water (about 100°F/38°C)

EQUIPMENT

Instant-read thermometer

16-cup (4 L) mixing bowl

Wooden spoon or Danish dough whisk

METHOD

1 Spoon the flour into a measuring cup, level with a knife or your finger, then dump the flour into the mixing bowl.

2 Add the sugar, yeast and salt to the flour. Stir together with a wooden spoon or Danish dough whisk. In a bowl, combine the butter and buttermilk. Add to the flour mixture, then add the eggs. Add the water and stir together until just moistened. Beat 40 strokes, scraping the bottom and the sides of the bowl, until the dough forms a lumpy, sticky mass.

3 Cover with plastic wrap and let rise at room temperature (72°F/22°C) in a draft-free place for 2 hours or until the dough has risen nearly to the top of the bowl and has a sponge-like appearance.

4 Use that day or place the dough, covered with plastic wrap, in the refrigerator for up to 3 days before baking.

TIP

Before storing the dough in the refrigerator, use a permanent marker to write the date on the plastic wrap, so you'll know when you made your dough — and when to use it up 3 days later.

BAKING WITH CANADIAN BREAD FLOUR

Canadian bread flour generally has a higher protein content than U.S. bread flour. That means it absorbs more water. If using Canadian bread flour, you may need to use slightly more water to avoid a dry dough. Begin by adding an extra tablespoon or two (15 to 30 mL) of water and continue adding until a soft dough is formed.

EASY ARTISAN BRIOCHE BREADS IN MINUTES A DAY

Day 1: Stir the dough together and let rise. Bake, or cover and chill.

Days 2–3: Remove part of the dough, form and bake.

Lemon-Scented Brioche Dough

Add 1 tbsp (15 mL) freshly grated lemon zest to the butter mixture.

Lemon-Poppy Seed Brioche Dough

Add 1 tbsp (15 mL) freshly grated lemon zest to the butter mixture. Grind ½ cup (125 mL) poppy seeds in a clean coffee or spice grinder and add to the butter mixture.

Orange-Scented Brioche Dough

Add 1 tbsp (15 mL) freshly grated orange zest to the butter mixture.

Butternut Brioche Dough

Makes enough dough for bread, rolls, savarins or beignets to serve 12 to 16

Traditional brioche turns even more golden — and a little less rich — when you add puréed cooked squash or pumpkin to the dough. Brush traditional brioche shapes with an egg wash before baking. You won't need the egg wash for breads, rolls, beignets or savarins that are to be glazed or dusted with sugar.

INGREDIENTS

6½ cups (1.625 L) unbleached bread flour or a mixture of bread and all-purpose flour

½ cup (125 mL) granulated sugar

2 tbsp (25 mL) instant or bread machine yeast

1½ tbsp (22 mL) fine kosher salt

1 cup (250 mL) unsalted butter, melted

½ cup (125 mL) buttermilk

8 eggs, beaten

1 cup (250 mL) puréed cooked butternut squash or pumpkin

¾ cup (175 mL) lukewarm water (about 100°F/38°C)

EQUIPMENT

Instant-read thermometer

16-cup (4 L) mixing bowl

Wooden spoon or Danish dough whisk

BAKING WITH CANADIAN BREAD FLOUR

Canadian bread flour generally has a higher protein content than U.S. bread flour. That means it absorbs more water. If using Canadian bread flour, you may need to use slightly more water to avoid a dry dough. Begin by adding an extra tablespoon or two (15 to 30 mL) of water and continue adding until a soft dough is formed.

METHOD

1 Spoon the flour into a measuring cup, level with a knife or your finger, then dump the flour into the mixing bowl.

2 Add the sugar, yeast and salt to the flour. Stir together with a wooden spoon or Danish dough whisk. In a bowl, combine the butter and buttermilk. Add to the flour mixture, then add the eggs. In another bowl, combine the squash and water. Add to the flour mixture and stir together until just moistened. Beat 40 strokes, scraping the bottom and the sides of the bowl, until the dough forms a lumpy, sticky mass.

3 Cover with plastic wrap and let rise at room temperature (72°F/22°C) in a draft-free place for 2 hours or until the dough has risen nearly to the top of the bowl and has a sponge-like appearance.

4 Use that day or place the dough, covered with plastic wrap, in the refrigerator for up to 3 days before baking.

TIP

To prepare the purée, simply cover frozen cubed butternut squash with water and cook until tender, then drain and purée in a food processor. Or, of course, you can use fresh squash, peeled, seeded, chopped and cooked until tender. One pound (500 g) of chopped peeled squash will yield about 1 cup (250 mL) puréed squash.

VARIATION

You can also use canned pumpkin purée (not pumpkin pie filling), canned puréed squash or puréed sweet potatoes (canned or fresh or frozen, cooked).

Brioche à Tête

Makes 1 loaf, to serve 12 to 16

This is the classic brioche shape, baked in a fluted metal mold and with a topknot of dough in the center of the loaf, but with a rustic exterior. The egg wash gives it a deliciously dark sheen to set off the mellow, honeycombed crumb. You'll get accolades when you proudly serve this with Artisan Butter (page 198) and your best jams and jellies. And more good news: leftover brioche is delicious as French toast or used in desserts as you would pound cake.

INGREDIENTS

½ recipe prepared Easy Artisan Brioche Dough (page 150), about the size of a volleyball

Unbleached all-purpose or bread flour

1 egg, lightly beaten with 1 tbsp (15 mL) water

3 cups (750 mL) hot water

EQUIPMENT

Large brioche pan, buttered

Broiler pan

Baking stone

METHOD

1 Place dough on a floured surface and dust very lightly with flour. Flour your hands. Pinch off a piece of dough the size of a tennis ball and roll into a teardrop shape. Working the dough as little as possible and adding flour as necessary, form the remaining dough into a round. With the handle of a wooden spoon or a bent pointing finger, make a depression in the center of the loaf, almost to the bottom. Place the small teardrop of dough, pointed end down, in the depression. Smooth the dough with your hands to form a soft, non-sticky skin. Pinch any seams together. Lightly flour any sticky places on the dough. The dough should feel soft and smooth all over, but not at all sticky.

2 Place the loaf in the prepared pan and brush with egg wash. Cover with a tea towel and let rest at room temperature for 40 minutes.

3 About 30 minutes before baking, place the broiler pan on the lower shelf and the baking stone on the middle shelf of the oven. Preheat to 400°F (200°C).

4 Carefully pull the middle rack of the oven out several inches. Place the brioche pan on the hot stone. Push the middle rack back in place. Pull the lower rack out, pour the hot water into the broiler pan and push the lower rack back in place. Close the oven door immediately so the steam will envelop the oven.

5 Bake for 55 to 60 minutes or until the crust is a medium dark brown and an instant-read thermometer inserted in the center of the loaf registers at least 190°F (90°C). Remove from pan and transfer to a rack to cool.

TIP

Enjoy right away or let cool completely, wrap and freeze for up to 3 months.

Individual Brioches

Makes 8 individual brioches

A basket of individual brioches, with their distinctively shiny topknots, can welcome friends and family to breakfast. Serve with Artisan Butter (page 198) and your best fruit preserves.

INGREDIENTS

$\frac{1}{2}$ recipe prepared Easy Artisan Brioche Dough (page 150), about the size of a volleyball

Unbleached all-purpose or bread flour

1 egg, lightly beaten with 1 tbsp (15 mL) water

3 cups (750 mL) hot water

EQUIPMENT

8 individual metal brioche pans or muffin cups, buttered

Broiler pan

Baking stone

METHOD

1 Place dough on a floured surface and dust very lightly with flour. Flour your hands. Working the dough as little as possible and adding flour as necessary, form the dough into an 8-inch (20 cm) cylinder. With a dough scraper, cut the dough into 1-inch (2.5 cm) slices. Roll each slice into a ball. Lightly flour any sticky places on the dough.

2 Place each ball in a prepared cup and brush with egg wash. Cover with a tea towel and let rest at room temperature for 40 minutes.

3 About 30 minutes before baking, place the broiler pan on the lower shelf and the baking stone on the middle shelf of the oven. Preheat to 400°F (200°C).

4 Carefully pull the middle rack of the oven out several inches. Place the brioche pans on the hot stone. Push the middle rack back in place. Pull the lower rack out, pour the hot water into the broiler pan and push the lower rack back in place. Close the oven door immediately so the steam will envelop the oven.

5 Bake for 15 to 18 minutes or until the crust is a medium dark brown and an instant-read thermometer inserted in the center of a roll registers at least 190°F (90°C). Remove from pan and transfer to a rack to cool.

TIP

Enjoy right away or let cool completely, wrap and freeze for up to 3 months.

Brioche Pull-Aparts

Makes 8 rolls

Whether simply brushed with softened butter or with a more flavorful filling (see variations, below), these feathery-crumbed pull-aparts will have you looking for an occasion to serve them.

INGREDIENTS

½ recipe prepared Easy Artisan Brioche Dough (page 150), about the size of a volleyball

Unbleached all-purpose or bread flour

¼ cup (50 mL) unsalted butter, softened

2 cups (500 mL) hot water for broiler pan

EQUIPMENT

Rolling pin

8-inch (20 cm) round cake pan, buttered

Broiler pan

Baking stone

METHOD

1 Place dough on a floured surface and dust very lightly with flour. Flour your hands and the rolling pin. Working the dough as little as possible and adding flour as necessary, roll out the dough into a 12- by 8-inch (30 by 20 cm) rectangle. Spread the butter over the dough, leaving a ½-inch (1 cm) perimeter. Starting with a short end, roll up the dough into a cylinder. If the dough begins to stick to the surface, use a dough scraper to push flour under the dough and scrape it up. Gently press and squeeze as you're rolling, to form the dough into a solid cylinder. With a pastry brush, brush off any excess flour. With the dough scraper, slice the cylinder into 1-inch (2.5 cm) pieces.

2 Place the rolls, cut side up, in the prepared pan so that they are almost touching. Cover with a tea towel and let rest at room temperature for 40 minutes.

3 About 30 minutes before baking, place the broiler pan on the lower shelf and the baking stone on the middle shelf of the oven. Preheat to 400°F (200°C).

4 Carefully pull the middle rack of the oven out several inches. Place the cake pan on the hot stone. Push the middle rack back in place. Pull the lower rack out, pour the hot water into the broiler pan and push the lower rack back in place. Close the oven door immediately so the steam will envelop the oven.

5 Bake for 32 to 34 minutes or until the crust is a medium dark brown and an instant-read thermometer inserted in the center of the rolls registers at least 190°F (90°C). Transfer to a wire rack to cool in pan.

VARIATIONS

You can also use Butternut Brioche Dough (page 152) or Lemon- or Orange-Scented Brioche Dough (variations, page 151).

Orange Brioche Pull-Aparts

Stir 1 tbsp (15 mL) granulated sugar and ½ tsp (2 mL) freshly grated orange zest into the butter.

Cinnamon Brioche Pull-Aparts

Sprinkle Cinnamon Sugar (page 210) over the butter on the dough.

Harvest Brioche Pull-Aparts

Makes 8 rolls

Spicy apple or pumpkin butters add just the right note to rich brioche.

INGREDIENTS

½ recipe prepared Butternut Brioche Dough (page 152), about the size of a volleyball

Unbleached all-purpose or bread flour

¼ cup (50 mL) apple or pumpkin butter

2 cups (500 mL) hot water for broiler pan

EQUIPMENT

Rolling pin

8-inch (20 cm) round cake pan, buttered

Broiler pan

Baking stone

METHOD

1 Place dough on a floured surface and dust very lightly with flour. Flour your hands and the rolling pin. Working the dough as little as possible and adding flour as necessary, roll out the dough into a 12- by 8-inch (30 by 20 cm) rectangle. Spread the apple butter over the dough, leaving a ½-inch (1 cm) perimeter. Starting with a short end, roll up the dough into a cylinder. If the dough begins to stick to the surface, use a dough scraper to push flour under the dough and scrape it up. Gently press and squeeze as you're rolling, to form the dough into a solid cylinder. With a pastry brush, brush off any excess flour. With the dough scraper, slice the cylinder into 1-inch (2.5 cm) pieces.

2 Place the rolls, cut side up, in the prepared pan so that they are almost touching. Cover with a tea towel and let rest at room temperature for 40 minutes.

3 About 30 minutes before baking, place the broiler pan on the lower shelf and the baking stone on the middle shelf of the oven. Preheat to 400°F (200°C).

4 Carefully pull the middle rack of the oven out several inches. Place the cake pan on the hot stone. Push the middle rack back in place. Pull the lower rack out, pour the hot water into the broiler pan and push the lower rack back in place. Close the oven door immediately so the steam will envelop the oven.

5 Bake for 32 to 34 minutes or until the crust is a medium dark brown and an instant-read thermometer inserted in the center of the rolls registers at least 190°F (90°C). Transfer to a wire rack to cool in pan.

Cider-Glazed Savarin

Makes 1 loaf, to serve 12 to 16

Classic French savarin is a rich dough baked in a ring mold, then glazed. With its soft, honeycombed crumb, it's delicious as a brunch dish or dessert. When you turn out the glazed, golden ring onto a serving plate, you can fill the center with sautéed apples, a bowl of flavored Artisan Butter (page 198), fresh fruit, a prepared fruit curd or whipped cream. For delicious variations, try serving Lemon-Scented Savarin with a bowl of lemon curd or Butternut Savarin with apple or pumpkin butter.

INGREDIENTS

½ recipe prepared Easy Artisan Brioche Dough (page 150), about the size of a volleyball

Unbleached all-purpose or bread flour

2 cups (500 mL) hot water

Cider Glaze with Rum (variation, page 213)

EQUIPMENT

4-cup (1 L) metal ring mold, buttered

Broiler pan

Baking stone

METHOD

1 Place dough on a floured surface and dust very lightly with flour. Working the dough as little as possible and adding flour as necessary, form the dough into a 14-inch (35 cm) cylinder. Lightly flour any sticky places on the dough. The dough should feel soft and smooth all over, but not at all sticky.

2 Place the dough in the prepared ring mold, pinching the ring of dough closed. Cover with a tea towel and let rest at room temperature for 40 minutes.

3 About 30 minutes before baking, place the broiler pan on the lower shelf and the baking stone on the middle shelf of the oven. Preheat to 425°F (220°C).

4 Carefully pull the middle rack of the oven out several inches. Place ring mold on the hot stone. Push the middle rack back in place. Pull the lower rack out, pour the hot water into the broiler pan and push the lower rack back in place. Close the oven door immediately so the steam will envelop the oven.

5 Bake for 8 minutes, then reduce the temperature to 350°F (180°C). Bake for 15 to 17 minutes or until the crust is a medium dark brown and an instant-read thermometer inserted in the center of the loaf registers at least 190°F (90°C). With a knife or spatula, loosen the savarin from the sides of the mold and turn out onto a wire rack set over a baking sheet. Poke holes all over the surface with a cake tester. Brush the savarin all over with glaze until it is all absorbed.

VARIATION

You can also use Butternut Brioche Dough (page 152).

Lemon-Scented Savarin

Use Lemon-Scented Brioche Dough (page 151) with Lemon or Cherry Glaze (page 213).

Orange-Scented Savarin

Use Orange-Scented Brioche Dough (page 151) with Orange Glaze (page 213).

Pan Dolce

Makes 1 large loaf, to serve 12

Bejeweled with dried fruits soaked in heady spirits, this festive sweet bread with a feathery crumb can be baked in a large, clean coffee can or a large brioche pan, or on coated panettone baking paper.

INGREDIENTS

2 cups (500 mL) mixed dried fruit, snipped into ½-inch (1 cm) pieces

½ cup (125 mL) lukewarm brandy, cognac, sherry or other fortified wine (about 100°F/38°C)

½ recipe prepared Easy Artisan Brioche Dough (page 150), about the size of a volleyball

Unbleached all-purpose or bread flour

2 cups (500 mL) hot water

Almond Glaze (variation, page 213)

Colored sprinkles

EQUIPMENT

Rolling pin

Large, clean metal coffee can, buttered; large metal brioche pan, buttered; or a large sheet of coated panettone baking paper

Broiler pan

Baking stone

METHOD

1 In a bowl, combine dried fruit and brandy; let stand for 30 minutes or until fruit is plump. Drain and pat dry.

2 Place dough on a floured surface and dust very lightly with flour. Flour your hands and the rolling pin. Working the dough as little as possible and adding flour as necessary, roll out the dough into a 12- by 6-inch (30 by 15 cm) oval. Lightly flour any sticky places on the dough. The dough should feel soft and smooth all over, but not at all sticky.

3 Arrange one-quarter of the fruit filling on the upper half of the dough oval and press into the dough with your hands. Fold the other half over the filling. Turn the dough a quarter turn. Working the dough as little as possible and adding flour as necessary, roll out the dough into an oval. Arrange another quarter of the fruit on the upper half of the oval and press into the dough with your hands. Fold the other half over the filling. Turn the dough a quarter turn. Working the dough as little as possible and adding flour as necessary, roll out the dough roll into an oval. Repeat this process twice more, sprinkling with flour as necessary, until all of the fruit has been incorporated into the dough. Form the dough into a ball and place in the prepared can or pan, or on the paper.

4 Cover with a tea towel and let rest at room temperature for 40 minutes.

5 About 30 minutes before baking, place the broiler pan on the lower shelf and the baking stone on the middle shelf of the oven. Preheat to 425°F (220°C).

6 Carefully pull the middle rack of the oven out several inches. Place the can, pan or paper on the hot stone. Push the middle rack back in place. Pull the lower rack out, pour the hot water into the broiler pan and push the lower rack back in place. Close the oven door immediately so the steam will envelop the oven.

7 Bake for 10 minutes, then reduce the temperature to 350°F (180°C). Bake for 35 to 40 minutes or until an instant-read thermometer inserted in the center of the loaf registers at least 190°F (90°C). Transfer to a wire rack set over a baking sheet to cool. When cool, remove from the can or pan (but leave on the paper) and place on the rack. Drizzle the top of the loaf with glaze so that it drips down the sides. Sprinkle with colored sprinkles.

Pocketbook Beignets

Makes 36 beignets

These delectable and habit-forming beignets will entice you to take it a step further and make these filled "pocketbook" fritters. To counteract the richness of fried brioche, use a very tart filling, such as apricot preserves, as at left, or orange marmalade or red currant jelly. Mix and match the finishing glaze with the filling.

INGREDIENTS

½ recipe prepared Easy Artisan Brioche Dough (page 150), about the size of a volleyball

Unbleached all-purpose or bread flour

¾ cup (175 mL) apricot preserves

Vegetable oil

Almond Glaze (variation, page 213)

EQUIPMENT

Rolling pin

Deep skillet or electric skillet

Candy/deep-fry thermometer

METHOD

1 Place dough on a floured surface and dust very lightly with flour. Flour your hands and the rolling pin. Working the dough as little as possible and adding flour as necessary, roll out the dough into a 12-inch (30 cm) square. With a pizza wheel or a sharp knife, cut the dough into 2-inch (5 cm) squares. Lightly dust each square with flour, if necessary, to keep it from being sticky. Place ½ tsp (2 mL) preserves in the center of each square. Draw up the sides of the dough and pinch closed. Loosely form into an egg or ball shape. Lightly dust with flour again, if necessary, to keep it from being sticky.

2 Cover with a tea towel and let rest at room temperature for 40 minutes.

3 In the skillet, heat 3 inches (7.5 cm) of oil over medium-high heat until it registers 350°F (180°C) on thermometer. Fry the pocketbook beignets, about six at a time, for about 1 minute per side or until golden brown. Using a slotted spoon, remove to a plate lined with paper towels to drain. While still warm, transfer to a wire rack placed over a baking sheet and drizzle with glaze.

VARIATIONS

Mix and match brioche doughs, finishing glazes, and fillings.

Orange Pocketbook Beignets

Use Orange-Scented Brioche Dough (variation, page 151), orange marmalade for the filling and Orange Glaze (variation, page 213).

Cranberry Orange Pocketbook Beignets

Use Orange-Scented Brioche Dough (variation, page 151), cranberry sauce for the filling and Orange Glaze (variation, page 213).

Cinnamon Apple Pocketbook Beignets

Use tart apple jelly for the filling and dust with Cinnamon Sugar (page 210).

Pumpkin Spice Pocketbook Beignets

Use Butternut Brioche Dough (page 152) and Spiced Pumpkin Butter (variation, page 198) for the filling, and dust with Cinnamon Sugar (page 210).

Part 3
MASTER BAKING

MASTER BAKING

We've gone from beginner through intermediate artisan baking, and now we're ready for recipes that use the skills you've learned: mixing and flavoring doughs, rolling and cutting, adding toppings and fillings, forming all the different shapes and artisan baking. The recipes and techniques in this chapter are for the dedicated amateur artisan baker — the person who wants an authentic bagel, flaky and buttery croissants that taste the way you get them in Paris, and a real Danish pastry.

Hungry? Intrigued? Then, let's take out the bowl and dough whisk again.

Easy Artisan Bagel Dough

Makes enough dough for bagels to serve 12 to 16

Bagels came to North America from Eastern Europe with Polish and German émigrés. The hallmarks of a good bagel are a shiny texture (from boiling them first) and a chewy crumb (from unbleached bread flour). The secret ingredient is barley malt, or malt syrup, a thick, dark brown sweetener made from sprouted barley. Bagel dough is easy to make, but the technique involved in forming the bagels takes a little practice. But even an imperfect homemade bagel is something to cheer!

INGREDIENTS

6½ cups (1.625 L) unbleached bread flour

2½ tbsp (32 mL) instant or bread machine yeast

1½ tbsp (22 mL) kosher salt

2 eggs, beaten

½ cup (125 mL) barley malt (malt syrup)

¼ cup (50 mL) vegetable oil

Hot water

EQUIPMENT

Instant-read thermometer

16-cup (4 L) mixing bowl

4-cup (1 L) glass measuring cup

Wooden spoon or Danish dough whisk

METHOD

1 Spoon the flour into a measuring cup, level with a knife or your finger, then dump the flour into the mixing bowl.

2 Add the yeast and salt to the flour. Stir together with a wooden spoon or Danish dough whisk. In the glass measuring cup, combine eggs, barley malt and oil. Pour in enough hot water to reach the 4-cup (1 L) mark and carefully whisk to blend. Pour into the flour mixture and stir together until just moistened. Beat 40 strokes, scraping the bottom and the sides of the bowl, until the dough forms a lumpy, sticky mass.

3 Cover the bowl with plastic wrap and let rise at room temperature (72°F/22°C) in a draft-free place for 2 hours or until the dough has risen nearly to the top of the bowl and has a sponge-like appearance.

4 Use that day or place the dough, covered with plastic wrap, in the refrigerator for up to 3 days before baking.

TIPS

- Look for barley malt in the syrup section at better grocery stores or health food shops, or online.
- Before storing the dough in the refrigerator, use a permanent marker to write the date on the plastic wrap, so you'll know when you made your dough — and when to use it up 3 days later.

Montreal Bagel Dough

Omit the salt. (You will also boil them in sweetened water and shape them smaller; see recipe, page 178.)

BAKING WITH CANADIAN BREAD FLOUR

Canadian bread flour generally has a higher protein content than U.S. bread flour. That means it absorbs more water. If using Canadian bread flour, you may need to use slightly more water to avoid a dry dough. Begin by adding an extra tablespoon or two (15 to 30 mL) of water and continue adding until a soft dough is formed.

BAGELS IN MINUTES A DAY

Day 1: Stir the dough together and let rise. Bake, or cover and chill.

Days 2–3: Remove part of the dough, form and bake bagels.

FLAVORING	HOW USED	FLAVOR
Caraway seeds	Mixed into dough	Caraway
Dehydrated onion flakes	Sprinkled on boiled bagels before baking	Toasted onion
Dill seeds	Sprinkled on boiled bagels before baking	Dill
Fennel seeds	Sprinkled on boiled bagels before baking	Licorice
Ground cinnamon	Mixed with sugar and sprinkled on dough before baking	Cinnamon
Nigella seeds	Sprinkled on boiled bagels before baking	Onion
Poppy seeds	Sprinkled on boiled bagels before baking	Sweet
Sesame seeds	Sprinkled on boiled bagels before baking	Sesame

Whole-Grain Bagel Dough

Makes enough dough for bagels to serve 12 to 16

INGREDIENTS

4½ cups (1.125 L) unbleached bread flour

2 cups (500 mL) whole-grain flour, such as white whole wheat

2½ tbsp (32 mL) instant or bread machine yeast

1½ tbsp (22 mL) kosher salt

1 tbsp (15 mL) Artisan Bread Dough Enhancer (page 194)

2 eggs, beaten

½ cup (125 mL) barley malt (malt syrup)

¼ cup (50 mL) vegetable oil

Hot water

EQUIPMENT

Instant-read thermometer

16-cup (4 L) mixing bowl

4-cup (1 L) glass measuring cup

Wooden spoon or Danish dough whisk

METHOD

1 One at a time, spoon the bread flour and whole-grain flour into a measuring cup, level with a knife or your finger, then dump into the mixing bowl. Combine well.

2 Add the yeast, salt and dough enhancer to the flours. Stir together with a wooden spoon or Danish dough whisk. In the glass measuring cup, combine eggs, barley malt and oil. Pour in enough hot water to reach the 4-cup (1 L) mark and carefully whisk to blend. Pour into the flour mixture and stir together until just moistened. Beat 40 strokes, scraping the bottom and the sides of the bowl, until the dough forms a lumpy, sticky mass.

3 Cover the bowl with plastic wrap and let rise at room temperature (72°F/22°C) in a draft-free place for 2 hours or until the dough has risen nearly to the top of the bowl and has a sponge-like appearance.

4 Use that day or place the dough, covered with plastic wrap, in the refrigerator for up to 3 days before baking.

TIPS

- Look for barley malt in the syrup section at better grocery stores or health food shops, or online.
- Before storing the dough in the refrigerator, use a permanent marker to write the date on the plastic wrap, so you'll know when you made your dough — and when to use it up 3 days later.

BAKING WITH CANADIAN BREAD FLOUR

Canadian bread flour generally has a higher protein content than U.S. bread flour. That means it absorbs more water. If using Canadian bread flour, you may need to use slightly more water to avoid a dry dough. Begin by adding an extra tablespoon or two (15 to 30 mL) of water and continue adding until a soft dough is formed.

Caraway Rye Bagel Dough

Makes enough dough for bagels to serve 12 to 16

INGREDIENTS

$4\frac{1}{2}$ cups (1.125 L) unbleached bread flour

2 cups (500 mL) rye flour

$2\frac{1}{2}$ tbsp (32 mL) instant or bread machine yeast

2 tbsp (25 mL) caraway seeds

$1\frac{1}{2}$ tbsp (22 mL) kosher salt

1 tbsp (15 mL) Artisan Bread Dough Enhancer (page 194)

2 eggs, beaten

$\frac{1}{2}$ cup (125 mL) barley malt (malt syrup)

$\frac{1}{4}$ cup (50 mL) vegetable oil

Hot water

EQUIPMENT

Instant-read thermometer

16-cup (4 L) mixing bowl

4-cup (1 L) glass measuring cup

Wooden spoon or Danish dough whisk

METHOD

1 One at a time, spoon the bread flour and rye flour into a measuring cup, level with a knife or your finger, then dump into the mixing bowl. Combine well.

2 Add the yeast, caraway seeds, salt and dough enhancer to the flours. Stir together with a wooden spoon or Danish dough whisk. In the glass measuring cup, combine eggs, barley malt and oil. Pour in enough hot water to reach the 4-cup (1 L) mark and carefully whisk to blend. Pour into the flour mixture and stir together until just moistened. Beat 40 strokes, scraping the bottom and the sides of the bowl, until the dough forms a lumpy, sticky mass.

3 Cover the bowl with plastic wrap and let rise at room temperature (72°F/22°C) in a draft-free place for 2 hours or until the dough has risen nearly to the top of the bowl and has a sponge-like appearance.

4 Use that day or place the dough, covered with plastic wrap, in the refrigerator for up to 3 days before baking.

TIPS

- Look for barley malt in the syrup section at better grocery stores or health food shops, or online.
- Before storing the dough in the refrigerator, use a permanent marker to write the date on the plastic wrap, so you'll know when you made your dough — and when to use it up 3 days later.

New York Bagels

Makes 8 large bagels

Artisan bagels look like they were freshly made by an artisan's hand — yours! They are imperfectly shaped, crinkly and wrinkly; in short, quite unlike their smooth mass-produced cousins. But the flavor and texture are truly authentic — and addictive. They're crisp-crusted, with the right amount of "bite" and chewier crumb that authentic bagels have. You boil them first, then bake. Note that bagels need 2 hours to rest before they are boiled and baked.

INGREDIENTS

1/2 recipe prepared Easy Artisan Bagel Dough (page 172), about the size of a volleyball

Unbleached bread flour

2 cups (500 mL) hot water

EQUIPMENT

Rolling pin

Large baking sheet, lined with parchment paper

Broiler pan

Baking stone

METHOD

1 Place dough on a floured surface and dust very lightly with flour. Flour your hands and the rolling pin. Working the dough as little as possible and adding flour as necessary, roll out the dough into a large rectangle. Fold the dough in half, turn a quarter turn and roll out again. Repeat three more times. Form the dough into an 8-inch (20 cm) cylinder. Smooth the dough with your hands to form a soft, non-sticky skin. Pinch any seams together. Cut the cylinder into 1-inch (2.5 cm) pieces. Lightly flour any sticky places on the dough. The dough should feel soft and smooth all over, but not at all sticky. With your hands, pull, stretch, squeeze and roll each portion into an 8- to 9-inch (20 to 23 cm) rope. Hold one end of each rope between your thumb and forefinger in the palm of your hand. Drape the rest of the rope around the back of your hand until the other end touches the end you're holding. Pinch and squeeze the ends together.

2 Place the bagels on the prepared baking sheet. With your fingers, neaten them up into a bagel shape, making sure they're 2 inches (5 cm) apart. Cover with a slightly moistened tea towel and let rest at room temperature for 2 hours.

3 About 30 minutes before baking, place the broiler pan on the lower shelf and the baking stone on the middle shelf of the oven. Preheat to 450°F (230°C). Bring a large pot of water to a boil over medium-high heat.

4 Using a slotted spoon or a metal pancake turner, place four bagels in the boiling water. Boil for 1 minute. Gently turn them over and boil for 1 minute. Drain well and return to the baking sheet, placing them 2 inches (5 cm) apart. Repeat with the remaining bagels.

5 Carefully pull the middle rack of the oven out several inches. Place the baking sheet on the hot stone. Push the middle rack back in place. Pull the lower rack out, pour the hot water into the broiler pan and push the lower rack back in place. Close the oven door immediately so the steam will envelop the oven.

6 Bake for 25 to 27 minutes or until the crust is a medium dark brown and an instant-read thermometer inserted in the center of the bagels registers at least 190°F (90°C). Transfer to a wire rack to cool on pan.

TIP

Artisan bagels taste best the same day they're made.

Poppy Seed Bagels

Sprinkle boiled bagels with poppy seeds before baking.

Salt Bagels

Sprinkle boiled bagels with coarse kosher or sea salt before baking.

Onion Bagels

Sprinkle boiled bagels with dehydrated onion flakes before baking.

Asiago Bagels

Sprinkle boiled bagels with shredded Asiago cheese before baking.

Sesame Bagels

Sprinkle boiled bagels with sesame seeds before baking.

Cinnamon Raisin Bagels

In a bowl, combine $\frac{1}{2}$ cup (125 mL) packed light or dark brown sugar and 1 tbsp (15 mL) ground cinnamon. Sprinkle this mixture onto the dough rectangle, leaving a 1-inch (2.5 cm) perimeter, then sprinkle with $\frac{1}{2}$ cup (125 mL) raisins before rolling the dough up into a cylinder.

Montreal Bagels

Makes 12 small bagels

Montreal bagels are made with a salt-free dough. They're smaller than New York bagels and are boiled in water sweetened with barley malt. Then they're usually baked in a wood-burning oven. To simulate that, I use hardwood chips meant for the grill or smoker. Note that bagels need 2 hours to rest before they are boiled and baked. Artisan bagels taste best the same day they're made. If using the wood chips, be sure your kitchen is well ventilated.

INGREDIENTS

½ recipe prepared Montreal Bagel Dough (variation, page 172), about the size of a volleyball

Unbleached bread flour

½ cup (125 mL) barley malt (malt syrup)

2 cups (500 mL) hot water

EQUIPMENT

Rolling pin

Large baking sheet, lined with parchment paper

Broiler pan

Baking stone

¼ cup (50 mL) fine dry hardwood chips, such as mesquite or apple, moistened with 2 tbsp (25 mL) water (optional)

METHOD

1. Place dough on a floured surface and dust very lightly with flour. Flour your hands and the rolling pin. Working the dough as little as possible and adding flour as necessary, roll out the dough into a large rectangle. Fold the dough in half, turn a quarter turn and roll out again. Repeat three more times. Form the dough into a 12-inch (30 cm) cylinder. Smooth the dough with your hands to form a soft, non-sticky skin. Pinch any seams together. Cut the cylinder into 1-inch (2.5 cm) pieces. Lightly flour any sticky places on the dough. The dough should feel soft and smooth all over, but not at all sticky. With your hands, pull, stretch, squeeze and roll each portion into a 6-inch (15 cm) rope. Hold one end of each rope between your thumb and forefinger in the palm of your hand. Drape the rest of the rope around the back of your hand until the other end touches the end you're holding. Pinch and squeeze the ends together.

2. Place the bagels on the prepared baking sheet. With your fingers, neaten them up into a bagel shape, making sure they're 2 inches (5 cm) apart. Cover with a slightly moistened tea towel and let rest at room temperature for 2 hours.

3. About 30 minutes before baking, place the broiler pan on the lower shelf and the baking stone on the middle shelf of the oven. Preheat to 450°F (230°C). For the wood-burning oven technique, place the moistened wood chips in a small metal pan next to the broiler pan on the lower shelf. They will start to smolder and release wisps of smoke. Bring a large pot of water, sweetened with the barley malt, to a boil over medium-high heat.

4. Using a slotted spoon or a metal pancake turner, place four bagels in the boiling water. Boil for 1 minute. Gently turn them over and boil for 1 minute. Drain well and return to the baking sheet, placing them 2 inches (5 cm) apart. Repeat with the remaining bagels.

5. Carefully pull the middle rack of the oven out several inches. Place the baking sheet on the hot stone. Push the middle rack back in place. Pull the lower rack out, pour the hot water into the broiler pan and push the lower rack back in place. Close the oven door immediately so the steam will envelop the oven.

6. Bake for 22 to 25 minutes or until the crust is a medium dark brown and an instant-read thermometer inserted in the center of the bagels registers at least 190°F (90°C). Transfer to a wire rack to cool on pan. Remove the smoldering wood chips from the oven, let cool completely, then discard.

Poppy Seed Bagels

Sprinkle boiled bagels with poppy seeds before baking.

Salt Bagels

Sprinkle boiled bagels with coarse kosher or sea salt before baking.

Onion Bagels

Sprinkle boiled bagels with dehydrated onion flakes before baking.

Asiago Bagels

Sprinkle boiled bagels with shredded Asiago cheese before baking.

Sesame Bagels

Sprinkle boiled bagels with sesame seeds before baking.

Easy Artisan Buttery Yeast Dough

Makes enough dough for pastries, braids and galettes to serve 16 to 24

Buttery Yeast Dough takes us a step or two beyond Easy Artisan Sweet Dough and Easy Artisan Brioche Dough, with filling and folding techniques picked up in previous chapters. This dough starts with what's known as the detrempe (a sweet yeast dough), to which you add a butter layer, or buerrage, to create a laminated dough, or one in which layers of butter create rich flakiness during baking. Traditional recipes have you pound cold butter into rectangles, a tricky proposition. This streamlined method cuts the butter in with some of the flour, as you would do for a pie crust. The buerrage is then rolled into the dough. A little orange juice in the detrempe adds a nuanced flavor note and helps cut some of the richness. Because the structure of this dough does best rolled into linear shapes, we'll stick to rectangles and avoid circles.

INGREDIENTS

Detrempe

2½ cups (625 mL) unbleached all-purpose flour

⅓ cup (75 mL) granulated sugar

1 tbsp (15 mL) instant or bread machine yeast

1 tsp (5 mL) kosher salt

½ cup (125 mL) milk (whole or 2%)

2 eggs, beaten

¼ cup (50 mL) freshly squeezed orange juice

Buerrage

1 cup (250 mL) unbleached all-purpose flour

1 cup (250 mL) cold unsalted butter, cut into 16 pieces

EQUIPMENT

Instant-read thermometer

16-cup (4 L) mixing bowl

Wooden spoon or Danish dough whisk

Pastry blender or food processor

Rolling pin

METHOD

1 Spoon the flour into a measuring cup, level with a knife or your finger, then dump the flour into the mixing bowl.

2 Add the sugar, yeast and salt to the flour. Stir together with a wooden spoon or Danish dough whisk. Pour in the milk. Whisk the eggs with the juice, then stir into the flour mixture just until moistened. Beat 40 strokes, scraping the bottom and the sides of the bowl, until the dough forms a lumpy, sticky mass.

3 Cover the bowl with plastic wrap and let rise at room temperature (72°F/22°C) in a draft-free place for 2 hours or until the dough has risen nearly to the top of the bowl and has a sponge-like appearance.

4 Place the dough, covered with plastic wrap, in the refrigerator for up to 3 days before baking. (For the best flavor, refrigerate for at least 8 hours or overnight.)

5 Place the flour in a bowl. Using the pastry blender, cut in butter until the butter is the size of small peas or smaller. (Or place the flour and butter in the food processor and pulse until the butter is the size of small peas or

smaller.) Do not overwork; you want the butter to stay cold and solid. Cover and refrigerate for at least 1 hour or for up to 1 day.

6 Place the dough on a floured surface and dust very lightly with flour. Flour your hands and the rolling pin. Working the dough as little as possible and adding flour as necessary, roll out the dough into an 18- by 12-inch (45 by 30 cm) rectangle, using a dough scraper and your hands to lift and help form the dough into an even rectangle with the long sides on your right and left. Sprinkle half the buerrage on the top two-thirds of the dough, leaving a 1½-inch (4 cm) border on the right and left sides. With your hands, lightly press the buerrage into the dough so it will stick. Fold the bottom third of the dough up and over some of the filling, like you're folding a business letter. Fold the top third of the dough down so the filling is completely covered and you have a 12- by 6-inch (30 by 15 cm) rectangle. Use your hands to scoop up stray buerrage and tuck it back under the dough, and to help form the dough into an even rectangle.

7 Turn the dough a quarter turn, lightly flouring under and on top of the dough as necessary, and roll out into an 18- by 12-inch (45 by 30 cm) rectangle with the long sides on your right and left. Repeat the process with the remaining buerrage. Wrap with plastic wrap and refrigerate for 30 minutes. Roll out the dough into a rectangle and fold like a business letter two more times. Use your hands to help form the dough into an even 12- by 6-inch (30 by 15 cm) rectangle of laminated dough. Lightly flour any sticky places on the dough. The dough should feel firm all over, with flattened pieces of butter visible within the dough, but not at all sticky.

8 Wrap the dough with plastic wrap and refrigerate for at least 30 minutes or for up to 24 hours before using.

TIP

It's very important to keep laminated doughs cold, so the butter layers stay intact. Use a marble pastry work surface, if possible, and work in a cool room.

Danish Pastry Dough

Add 1½ tsp (7 mL) vanilla extract to the milk. (You can also add ½ tsp (2 mL) each ground cardamom and grated orange zest to the flour mixture.

CROISSANTS AND DANISH PASTRY IN MINUTES A DAY

Day 1: Make the detrempe and the buerrage. Cover and refrigerate.
Day 2: Roll the detrempe and buerrage together for laminated dough. Cover and refrigerate.
Day 3: Roll out the dough, cut and form into shapes. Cover and refrigerate, or let rise and bake.
Day 4: Let rise and (optional) bake.

Flaky, Buttery Croissants

Makes 20 croissants

INGREDIENTS

1 recipe prepared Easy Artisan Buttery Yeast Dough (page 180)

Unbleached all-purpose flour

1 egg, lightly beaten with 1 tbsp (15 mL) water

2 cups (500 mL) hot water

EQUIPMENT

Rolling pin

2 large baking sheets, lined with parchment paper

Broiler pan

Baking stone

METHOD

1 Remove the dough rectangle from the refrigerator and cut in half. Rewrap one half and return to the refrigerator. Transfer the other half to a generously floured surface and dust very lightly with flour. Flour your hands and the rolling pin. Roll out the dough to a 15- by 6-inch (38 by 15 cm) rectangle with the long sides horizontal. The dough should feel cold, firm and smooth all over, but not at all sticky. With a paring knife or pizza wheel, starting at a short side, mark the top and bottom of the dough at 3-inch (7.5 cm) intervals. From the left-hand edge of the bottom, make a diagonal cut up to the first 3-inch (7.5 cm) mark to form a long triangle with a 3-inch (7.5 cm) base at the top. Make another diagonal cut down to reach the next 3-inch (7.5 cm) mark at the bottom, creating another triangle. Repeat the process until you have 10 triangles. Lift each triangle and gently press and pull the top and down along the length of the triangle to stretch the base to 4 to 5 inches (10 to 12.5 cm) wide. Starting at the base, tightly roll each triangle into a crescent, stretching and pulling it as you go. Repeat the process with the remaining dough.

2 Place croissants 2 inches (5 cm) apart on the prepared baking sheets, arranging them so that the pointed tip is visible. Cover the baking sheets with plastic wrap and refrigerate for up to 24 hours, or let rise in a warm (72°F/22°C) place for 2 hours or until about doubled in size. (If chilling first, let the croissants come to room temperature, then let rise.)

3 About 30 minutes before baking, place the broiler pan on the lower shelf and the baking stone on the middle shelf of the oven. Preheat to 400°F (200°C).

4 Brush the croissants with egg wash.

5 Carefully pull the middle rack of the oven out several inches. Place one of the baking sheets on the hot stone. Push the middle rack back in place. Pull the lower rack out, pour the hot water into the broiler pan and push the lower rack back in place. Close the oven door immediately so the steam will envelop the oven.

6 Bake for 8 to 10 minutes or until the pastry is golden brown. Transfer to a wire rack to cool on pan. Repeat the baking process with the remaining croissants. Enjoy right away or let cool, wrap and freeze for up to 3 months.

TIPS

- It's very important to keep laminated doughs cold, so the butter layers stay intact. Use a marble pastry work surface, if possible, and work in a cool room. The dough should be at a warm room temperature only during the final rise.
- If you like, add a ribbon of Easy Artisan Glaze to finish.

VARIATION

You can use Danish Pastry Dough (page 181).

Danish Orange Pinwheels

Makes 32 pinwheels

INGREDIENTS

1 recipe prepared Danish Pastry Dough (variation, page 180)

Unbleached all-purpose flour

1 cup (250 mL) Orange Cream Cheese Filling (variation, page 206), softened

1 egg, lightly beaten with 1 tbsp (15 mL) water

2 cups (500 mL) hot water

Orange Glaze (variation, page 213)

EQUIPMENT

Rolling pin

2 large baking sheets, lined with parchment paper

Broiler pan

Baking stone

METHOD

1 Remove the dough rectangle from the refrigerator and cut in half. Rewrap one half and return to the refrigerator. Transfer the other half to a generously floured surface and dust very lightly with flour. Flour your hands and the rolling pin. Roll out the dough to a 12-inch (30 cm) square. The dough should feel cold, firm and smooth all over, but not at all sticky. With a sharp knife or pizza wheel, cut the dough into sixteen 3-inch (7.5 cm) squares. Place a generous teaspoon (7 mL) filling in the center of each square. Bring each corner of the square up and over the filling to meet in the middle and pinch them closed with your fingers. Repeat the process with the remaining dough.

2 Chill or rise. Place the pinwheels 2 inches (5 cm) apart on the prepared baking sheets. Cover the baking sheets with plastic wrap and refrigerate for up to 24 hours, or let rise in a warm (72°F/22°C) place for 2 hours or until about doubled in size. (If chilling first, let the pinwheels come to room temperature, then let rise.)

3 About 30 minutes before baking, place the broiler pan on the lower shelf and the baking stone on the middle shelf of the oven. Preheat to 400°F (200°C).

4 Brush with egg wash. Brush the pinwheels with egg wash.

5 Carefully pull the middle rack of the oven out several inches. Place one of the baking sheets on the hot stone. Push the middle rack back in place. Pull the lower rack out, pour the hot water into the broiler pan and push the lower rack back in place. Close the oven door immediately so the steam will envelop the oven.

6 Bake for 10 to 12 minutes or until the pastry is golden brown. Transfer to a wire rack set over a baking sheet and let cool on pan for 5 minutes, then drizzle with glaze. Repeat the baking process with the remaining pinwheels. Enjoy right away or let cool, wrap and freeze for up to 3 months.

TIPS

- It's very important to keep laminated doughs cold, so the butter layers stay intact. Use a marble pastry work surface, if possible, and work in a cool room. Only keep the dough at warm room temperature during the final rise.
- You can freeze baked pinwheels in plastic freezer bags for up to 3 months. To thaw, place frozen pastries on a baking sheet, cover lightly with foil and warm in a 350°F (180°C) oven for 15 minutes.

VARIATION

You can also use Easy Artisan Buttery Yeast Dough (page 180).

Danish Almond Plait

Makes 2 braided pastries, to serve 24

Not only does this long, braided pastry look terribly impressive on a breakfast or brunch table, but it's also easy to make. All you do, really, is crisscross fingers of dough over the central filling, and it looks like you worked all day.

INGREDIENTS

1 recipe prepared Easy Artisan Buttery Yeast Dough (page 180)

Unbleached all-purpose flour

Danish Almond Filling (page 204)

1 egg, lightly beaten with 1 tbsp (15 mL) water

Pearl sugar, white sanding sugar or coarse sugar

2 cups (500 mL) hot water

EQUIPMENT

Rolling pin

Flexible cutting board

Large baking sheet, lined with parchment paper

Broiler pan

Baking stone

METHOD

1 Remove the dough rectangle from the refrigerator and cut in half. Rewrap one half and return to the refrigerator. Transfer the other half to a generously floured surface and dust very lightly with flour. Flour your hands and the rolling pin. Roll out the dough to an 18- by 14-inch (45 by 35 cm) rectangle with the long sides to the left and right. The dough should feel cold, firm and smooth all over, but not at all sticky. Spoon half the filling down the center of the rectangle, leaving a 2-inch (5 cm) perimeter. With a paring knife or a pizza wheel, cut a diagonal line from the right side of the bottom of the filling through the dough to the end. Cut a diagonal line from the left side of the bottom of the filling through the dough to the end. Fold the resulting trapezoid of dough up and over the filling. Repeat with the top of the dough. Cut the pastry on either side of the filling into diagonal strips about $\frac{1}{2}$ inch (1 cm) wide. Fold the strips over the filling, alternating strips from each side, to create a braid effect, brushing away excess flour with a pastry brush. Trim any ends and gently press the braided dough together. Repeat the process with the remaining dough.

2 Using a flexible cutting board, scoop under each pastry and carefully transfer to the prepared baking sheet. Cover the baking sheet with plastic wrap and refrigerate for up to 24 hours, or let rise in a warm (72°F/22°C) place for 2 hours or until about doubled in size. (If chilling first, let the pastry come to room temperature, then let rise.)

3 About 30 minutes before baking, place the broiler pan on the lower shelf and the baking stone on the middle shelf of the oven. Preheat to 400°F (200°C).

4 Gently brush the pastry with egg wash and sprinkle with sugar.

5 Carefully pull the middle rack of the oven out several inches. Place the baking sheet on the hot stone. Push the middle rack back in place. Pull the lower rack out, pour the hot water into the broiler pan and push the lower rack back in place. Close the oven door immediately so the steam will envelop the oven.

6 Bake for 15 to 17 minutes or until the top of the pastry is deep brown and the rest is puffed and golden. Transfer to a wire rack to cool on pan. Enjoy right away or let cool, wrap and freeze for up to 3 months.

TIPS

- It's very important to keep laminated doughs cold, so the butter layers stay intact. Use a marble pastry work surface, if possible, and work in a cool room. The dough should be at a warm room temperature only during the final rise.
- Both pearl sugar and white sanding sugar are available at baking supply shops or online.

VARIATION

Danish Pastry Dough (variation, page 180).

Caramel Apple Plait

Use Caramel Apple Filling (page 202) in place of the Danish Almond Filling.

Sweet Cream Cheese Plait

Use Sweet Cream Cheese Filling (page 206) in place of the Danish Almond Filling. Serve each slice with fruit compote.

Danish Bear Claws

Makes 16 bear claws

Bear claws start out as squares. Then they're filled, folded and cut so that the edge of the pastry resembles stubby toes, which separate and spread out during baking. These pastries also get a drizzle of glaze at the end.

INGREDIENTS

1 recipe prepared Danish Pastry Dough (variation, page 180)

Unbleached all-purpose flour

$\frac{1}{2}$ cup (125 mL) apricot, cherry or plum preserves or Danish Almond Filling (page 204)

1 egg, lightly beaten with 1 tbsp (15 mL) water

2 cups (500 mL) hot water

Easy Artisan Glaze (page 212)

EQUIPMENT

Rolling pin

2 large baking sheets, lined with parchment paper

Broiler pan

Baking stone

METHOD

1 Remove the dough rectangle from the refrigerator and cut in half. Rewrap one half and return to the refrigerator. Transfer the other half to a generously floured surface and dust very lightly with flour. Flour your hands and the rolling pin. Roll out the dough to a 16- by 8-inch (40 by 20 cm) rectangle. The dough should feel cold, firm and smooth all over, but not at all sticky. With a paring knife or pizza wheel, cut the dough into eight 4-inch (10 cm) squares. Mound 2 tsp (10 mL) preserves in the center of each square. Brush one side of each square with egg wash, then fold the opposite side over the filling, pressing the edges together to seal. Make three cuts on the folded side, almost but not quite to the seam side. Repeat the process with the remaining dough.

2 Place the bear claws 2 inches (5 cm) apart on the prepared baking sheets. Gently fan the "toes" slightly. Cover the baking sheets with plastic wrap and refrigerate for up to 24 hours, or let rise in a warm (72°F/22°C) place for 2 hours or until about doubled in size. (If chilling first, let the bear claws come to room temperature, then let rise.)

3 About 30 minutes before baking, place the broiler pan on the lower shelf and the baking stone on the middle shelf of the oven. Preheat to 400°F (200°C).

4 Brush the bear claws with egg wash.

5 Carefully pull the middle rack of the oven out several inches. Place one of the baking sheets on the hot stone. Push the middle rack back in place. Pull the lower rack out, pour the hot water into the broiler pan and push the lower rack back in place. Close the oven door immediately so the steam will envelop the oven.

6 Bake for 10 to 12 minutes or until the pastry is golden brown. Transfer to a wire rack set over a baking sheet and let cool on pan for 5 minutes, then drizzle with glaze. Repeat with remaining pastry.

TIP

It's very important to keep laminated doughs cold, so the butter layers stay intact. Use a marble pastry work surface, if possible, and work in a cool room. Only keep the dough at warm room temperature during the final rise.

Caramel Apple Galettes

Makes 8 galettes

It's very important to keep laminated doughs cold, so the butter layers stay intact. Use a marble pastry work surface, if possible, and work in a cool room. Only keep the dough at warm room temperature during the final rise.

INGREDIENTS

$\frac{1}{2}$ recipe prepared Easy Artisan Buttery Yeast Dough (page 180)

Unbleached all-purpose flour

1 egg, lightly beaten with 1 tbsp (15 mL) water

1 cup (250 mL) Caramel Apple Filling (page 202)

$\frac{1}{4}$ cup (50 mL) chopped pecans or sliced almonds

2 cups (500 mL) hot water

EQUIPMENT

Rolling pin

Large baking sheet, lined with parchment paper

Broiler pan

Baking stone

METHOD

1. Place dough on a generously floured surface and dust very lightly with flour. Flour your hands and the rolling pin. Roll out the dough to a 16- by 8-inch (40 by 20 cm) rectangle. The dough should feel cold, firm and smooth all over, but not at all sticky. With a sharp knife or a pizza wheel, cut the dough into 4-inch (10 cm) squares.

2. Chill or rise. Place the squares 2 inches (5 cm) apart on the prepared baking sheet. Cover the baking sheet with plastic wrap and refrigerate for up to 24 hours, or let rise in a warm (72°F/22°C) place for 2 hours or until about doubled in size. (If chilling first, let the galettes come to room temperature, then let rise.)

3. About 30 minutes before baking, place the broiler pan on the lower shelf and the baking stone on the middle shelf of the oven. Preheat to 425°F (220°C).

4. Add topping. Brush the pastry squares with egg wash. Spoon 2 tbsp (25 mL) Caramel Apple Filling in the center of each square. Sprinkle with pecans.

5. Carefully pull the middle rack of the oven out several inches. Place the baking sheet on the hot stone. Push the middle rack back in place. Pull the lower rack out, pour the hot water into the broiler pan and push the lower rack back in place. Close the oven door immediately so the steam will envelop the oven.

6. Bake for 8 minutes, then reduce the temperature to 350°F (180°C). Bake for 10 to 12 minutes or until the pastry is golden brown. Transfer to a wire rack to cool on pan. Enjoy right away or let cool, wrap and freeze for up to 3 months.

VARIATION

You can also use Danish Pastry Dough (variation, page 180).

Berries 'n' Cream Galettes

Makes 8 galettes

It's very important to keep laminated doughs cold, so the butter layers stay intact. Use a marble pastry work surface, if possible, and work in a cool room. Only keep the dough at warm room temperature during the final rise.

INGREDIENTS

$\frac{1}{2}$ recipe prepared Easy Artisan Buttery Yeast Dough (page 274)

Unbleached all-purpose flour

1 egg, lightly beaten with 1 tbsp (15 mL) water

1 cup (250 mL) Sweet Cream Cheese Filling (page 206)

$\frac{1}{4}$ cup (50 mL) fresh berries

$\frac{1}{4}$ cup (50 mL) sliced almonds

2 cups (500 mL) hot water

EQUIPMENT

Rolling pin

Large baking sheet, lined with parchment paper

Broiler pan

Baking stone

METHOD

1 Place dough on a generously floured surface and dust very lightly with flour. Flour your hands and the rolling pin. Roll out the dough to a 16- by 8-inch (40 by 20 cm) rectangle. The dough should feel cold, firm and smooth all over, but not at all sticky. With a sharp knife or a pizza wheel, cut the dough into 4-inch (10 cm) squares.

2 Place the squares 2 inches (5 cm) apart on the prepared baking sheet. Cover the baking sheet with plastic wrap and refrigerate for up to 24 hours, or let rise in a warm (72°F/22°C) place for 2 hours or until about doubled in size. (If chilling first, let the galettes come to room temperature, then let rise.)

3 About 30 minutes before baking, place the broiler pan on the lower shelf and the baking stone on the middle shelf of the oven. Preheat to 425°F (220°C).

4 Brush the pastry squares with egg wash. Spoon 2 tbsp (25 mL) Sweet Cream Cheese Filling in the center of each square. Sprinkle with berries and almonds.

5 Carefully pull the middle rack of the oven out several inches. Place the baking sheet on the hot stone. Push the middle rack back in place. Pull the lower rack out, pour the hot water into the broiler pan and push the lower rack back in place. Close the oven door immediately so the steam will envelop the oven.

6 Bake for 8 minutes, then reduce the temperature to 350°F (180°C). Bake for 10 to 12 minutes or until the pastry is golden brown. Transfer to a wire rack to cool on pan. Enjoy right away or let cool, wrap and freeze for up to 3 months.

VARIATION

You can also use Danish Pastry Dough (variation, page 180).

Artisan Bread Dough Enhancer

Makes about $1\frac{3}{4}$ cups (425 mL)

Dough enhancer contains ingredients that help heavy doughs rise better and unbleached all-purpose flour do the heavy lifting of bread flour. So if bread flour is not always available in your area, make a batch of dough enhancer and keep it in a tightly closed jar in your refrigerator. To increase the level of protein in unbleached all-purpose flour so you can use it in place of bread flour, add 1 tsp (5 mL) Artisan Bread Dough Enhancer to each cup (250 mL) of all-purpose flour. However, you'll need to search for dough enhancer ingredients. Boxes of vital wheat gluten, nonfat dry milk and ground ginger are available in the baking aisle. Unflavored gelatin is with puddings and gelatin mixes. Boxes of pectin and ascorbic acid are available where canning and preserving items are shelved; ascorbic acid is sometimes also shelved with Jewish foods. Soy-lecithin granules (Bob's Red Mill brand is one) can be found in the baking or health foods aisle. You can also buy ready-made powdered dough enhancer in the baking aisle of better grocery stores.

INGREDIENTS

1 cup (250 mL) vital wheat gluten

$\frac{1}{2}$ cup (125 mL) instant nonfat dry milk powder

2 tbsp (25 mL) soy-lecithin granules

2 tbsp (25 mL) powdered pectin

2 tbsp (25 mL) unflavored gelatin powder

1 tsp (5 mL) ground ginger

1 tsp (5 mL) ascorbic acid crystals

METHOD

1 In a glass jar, combine gluten, dry milk, soy-lecithin granules, pectin, gelatin, ginger and ascorbic acid crystals. Close the lid and shake to blend. Keeps, refrigerated, indefinitely.

Rosemary Walnuts

Makes about 2 cups (500 mL)

For years, my BBQ Queen co-author, Karen Adler, has been making roasted rosemary walnuts for the holidays. As I was experimenting with easy techniques for artisan breads, I put two and two together: wouldn't those walnuts taste great in bread? Fold this mixture into bread dough, as instructed in Easy Artisan Seeded and Filled Dough (page 76), and into slow-rise and naturally leavened doughs as well.

INGREDIENTS

2 tsp (10 mL) crushed dried rosemary

1/2 tsp (2 mL) kosher salt

1/2 tsp (2 mL) cayenne pepper

2 tbsp (25 mL) unsalted butter

2 cups (500 mL) walnut halves

EQUIPMENT

Baking sheet, lined with parchment paper

Preheat oven to 400°F (200°C)

METHOD

1 In a small bowl, stir together rosemary, salt and cayenne until well blended, with no lumps or clumps.

2 In a large saucepan, melt butter over medium-high heat. Stir in the rosemary mixture. Add walnuts and stir for 2 to 3 minutes or until evenly coated.

3 Using a spatula, spread walnuts on prepared baking sheet. Bake in preheated oven for 10 to 15 minutes or until walnuts are lightly toasted but not burned.

4 Let cool, use right away or store in an airtight container at room temperature for up to 2 months.

Easy Caramelized Onions

Makes about 2 cups (500 mL)

Who doesn't like caramelized onions? They're so adaptable as pizza and flatbread toppings, and savory roll and sandwich fillings, that you just have to have a batch on hand in the refrigerator or freezer. This recipe is adapted from one by Kathryn Moore and Roxanne Wyss (www.pluggedintocooking.com), and it's fabulous.

INGREDIENTS

4 large onions, thinly sliced

2 tbsp (25 mL) olive oil

2 tbsp (25 mL) unsalted butter

Salt and freshly ground black pepper

METHOD

1. In a small (2- to 4-quart) slow cooker, combine onions, oil and butter. Cover and cook on High for 6 to 8 hours or until onions are medium brown and wilted. Season to taste with salt and pepper. Let cool.

2. Use right away or transfer to an airtight container and refrigerate for up to 1 week or freeze for up to 3 months.

TIP

For caramelized onions on the stovetop, heat the oil and butter in a large saucepan over medium-low heat. Stir in the onions and cook, stirring occasionally, for 20 to 30 minutes or until the onions have caramelized. Season to taste with salt and pepper.

Caramelized Shallots and Garlic with Red Wine

Makes about 3 cups (750 mL)

As a topping for artisan flatbreads, this heady mixture shines. Serve with a good red wine and artisan cheese as an appetizer or a snack.

INGREDIENTS

2 tbsp (25 mL) olive oil

25 small shallots

20 cloves garlic

2 tbsp (25 mL) granulated sugar

3 cups (750 mL) dry red wine, divided

Coarse salt and freshly ground black pepper

METHOD

1 In a large skillet, heat oil over medium-high heat. Add shallots and garlic; cook, stirring occasionally, for about 10 minutes or until shallots are golden brown. Add sugar, stir well and cook for about 4 minutes or until sugar caramelizes. Add 2 cups (500 mL) of the wine, reduce heat to low, cover and simmer for 20 to 25 minutes or until shallots are soft. Add the remaining wine and simmer, uncovered, for 10 to 15 minutes or until wine has evaporated. Season to taste with salt and pepper. Let cool.

2 Use right away or transfer to an airtight container and refrigerate for up to 5 days.

Artisan Butter

Makes about 1 cup (250 mL)

Farm wives used to make their spending money by churning butter by hand to sell at the market. We can count ourselves fortunate that the food processor now takes the place of the old wooden churn in the home kitchen. If you're making Easy Artisan bread, you should also serve delicious but equally artisan butter, and this is it. This recipe produces unsalted butter; if you like, add sea salt to taste. Ultra-pasteurized cream will take a little longer to process, but still makes delicious butter.

INGREDIENT

2 cups (500 mL) heavy or whipping (35%) cream

METHOD

1 Line a sieve with a single layer of cheesecloth or a clean terrycloth tea towel and place the sieve over a bowl. Pour the cream into the food processor and process for about 5 minutes. The cream will go, in stages, from liquid to whipped cream to thick whipped cream to a solid mass of butter that separates from the milky liquid, or whey.

2 Transfer the butter to the lined sieve and press the butter with a wooden spoon or spatula to release more of the whey. When the butter does not release any more whey, scoop it from the sieve and cover with plastic wrap.

3 Use right away, keep covered in the refrigerator for up to 1 month or freeze indefinitely.

Garlic Herb Butter

In a bowl, combine 1 cup (250 mL) softened butter with 1 large clove garlic, minced, and 2 tbsp (25 mL) mixed chopped fresh herbs, such as flat-leaf (Italian) parsley, dill, tarragon, chives, oregano and/or rosemary, or to taste.

Savory Whipped Onion Butter

In a food processor, combine 1 cup (250 mL) softened butter, ¼ cup (50 mL) minced onion, ¼ cup (50 mL) minced flat-leaf (Italian) parsley, 2 tsp (10 mL) Worcestershire sauce, ½ tsp (2 mL) dry mustard and ½ tsp (2 mL) cracked black pepper; process until light and fluffy.

Honey Butter

In a bowl, combine 1 cup (250 mL) softened butter with 1 tbsp (15 mL) medium-colored liquid clover or wildflower honey, or to taste.

Raspberry Butter

In a bowl, combine 1 cup (250 mL) softened butter with 1 cup (250 mL) mashed fresh or thawed frozen raspberries. (Or use strawberries for Strawberry Butter.)

Spiced Pumpkin Butter

In a bowl, combine 1 cup (250 mL) softened butter with ⅓ cup (75 mL) canned pumpkin purée (not pie filling), 1 tsp (5 mL) grated orange zest and 1 tsp (5 mL) pumpkin pie spice.

Pomegranate Orange Butter

In a bowl, combine 1 cup (250 mL) softened butter with ¼ cup (50 mL) pomegranate molasses and 1 tbsp (15 mL) grated orange zest.

Honey Spice Applesauce

Makes about 4 cups (1 L)

Dark with spices, this applesauce is wonderful served warm with artisan bread or as a topping for Apple Custard Kuchen (page 146).

INGREDIENTS

4 cups (1 L) unsweetened applesauce

1 cup (250 mL) clover or other mild honey

2 tsp (10 mL) ground cinnamon

1/4 tsp (1 mL) freshly grated nutmeg

1/4 tsp (1 mL) kosher salt, or to taste

1 tsp (5 mL) freshly squeezed lemon juice, or to taste

METHOD

1. In a large saucepan, heat applesauce, honey, cinnamon and nutmeg over medium-high heat until bubbling. Reduce heat and simmer for 5 minutes or until thickened. Taste, then add salt and lemon juice as needed.

2. Use right away or let cool, transfer to airtight containers and freeze for up to 6 months.

Caramel Apple Filling

Makes about 2 cups (500 mL)

As a filling for pull-aparts, coffee cakes, swirled loaves, tea rings, Danish pastries or croissants, this has no peer. After you make it, the problem will be disciplining yourself to try only a little taste and save the rest for the recipe.

INGREDIENTS

1/4 cup (50 mL) unsalted butter

1/2 cup (125 mL) packed light or dark brown sugar

4 large tart apples (such as Granny Smith or Fuji), peeled and cut into small dice

Freshly squeezed lemon juice

METHOD

1 In a large skillet, melt butter over medium-high heat. Stir in brown sugar until well blended. Stir in apples and cook, stirring, for about 12 minutes or until softened. Remove from heat and stir in lemon juice to taste. Let cool completely.

2 Use right away once cool, or transfer to an airtight container and refrigerate for up to 3 days.

Poppy Seed Filling

Makes about 1 cup (250 mL)

Artisan bakers of Polish and Slavic descent love the combination of sweet, crunchy poppy seeds and tart lemon in festive breads and pastries. Polish bakeries often sell bags of poppy seeds already ground, but it's easy to do at home.

INGREDIENTS

1 cup (250 mL) poppy seeds

$\frac{1}{2}$ cup (125 mL) milk

2 tbsp (25 mL) granulated sugar

1 tbsp (15 mL) honey

1 tsp (5 mL) ground allspice

METHOD

1. Grind the poppy seeds, in batches if necessary, in a clean coffee grinder, spice grinder or small food processor, or by hand using a mortar and pestle.

2. In a saucepan, combine ground poppy seeds, milk, sugar, honey and allspice; bring to a boil over medium-high heat. Reduce heat and simmer for 10 minutes, stirring frequently, until sugar and honey are well dissolved and the mixture has thickened slightly. Remove from the heat and let cool.

3. Use right away or transfer to an airtight container and refrigerate for up to 1 week.

Danish Almond Filling

Makes about 2½ cups (625 mL)

Midwesterners of Scandinavian descent love a vanilla-scented almond filling. If you prefer a stronger almond flavoring, use the almond extract. This filling tastes best if it has several days to mature.

INGREDIENTS

8 oz (250 g) sliced almonds (about 1½ cups/375 mL)

1 cup (250 mL) granulated sugar

1 tsp (5 mL) almond or vanilla extract

2 egg whites

METHOD

1. Preheat oven to 300°F (150°C).

2. Spread almonds in a single layer on a baking sheet. Toast in preheated oven for 10 to 15 minutes or until nuts are golden and have a toasty aroma. (Check after 10 minutes, and do not let brown.) Let cool, then discard any nuts that have turned dark brown.

3. In a food processor or blender, grind cooled almonds to a fine paste. Add sugar and process until the mixture resembles coarse flour. Add almond extract and egg whites; process for 2 to 3 minutes or until a stiff paste forms.

4. Transfer to an airtight container and refrigerate until ready to use, up to 3 days.

TIP

Toasting the nuts first gives this filling a better flavor.

Toasted Hazelnut Filling

Substitute hazelnuts for the almonds and rub off the skins after toasting. Omit the extract.

Pistachio Filling

Substitute unsalted roasted pistachios for the almonds and skip Step 1. Use almond extract.

Pure Almond Extract
Extrait d'amande pur

Sweet Cream Cheese Filling

Makes about 1⅓ cups (325 mL)

Delicious as a filling for pull-aparts, crescent rolls, Danish pastries or coffee cake, or swirled loafs, this cream cheese mixture can be flavored in many different ways (see variations, at right).

INGREDIENTS

1 package (8 oz/250 g) cream cheese, softened

1 egg yolk

¼ cup (50 mL) granulated sugar

2 tbsp (25 mL) all-purpose flour

1 tsp (5 mL) vanilla extract

METHOD

1. In a food processor, combine cream cheese, egg yolk, sugar, flour and vanilla; process until smooth.
2. Use right away or transfer to an airtight container and refrigerate for up to 3 days.

Almond Cream Cheese Filling

Use 1 tsp (5 mL) almond extract in place of the vanilla.

Lemon Cream Cheese Filling

Use 1 tsp (5 mL) lemon extract or grated lemon zest in place of the vanilla.

Orange Cream Cheese Filling

Use 1 tsp (5 mL) orange extract or grated orange zest in place of the vanilla.

Sweet Spice Cream Cheese Filling

Add 1 tsp (5 mL) apple pie spice.

Coconut Cream Cheese Filling

Add ½ cup (125 mL) sweetened flaked coconut.

Cinnamon Filling

Makes about $\frac{3}{4}$ cup (175 mL)

This is the classic filling for cinnamon rolls, Swedish tea rings and other pastries. This mild version uses granulated sugar and regular grocery-store cinnamon (usually from Indonesia).

INGREDIENTS

6 tbsp (90 mL) granulated sugar

2 tbsp (25 mL) ground cinnamon

$\frac{3}{4}$ cup (175 mL) unsalted butter, softened

METHOD

1. In a bowl, combine sugar and cinnamon. Using a fork, beat in butter until smooth and well blended.

VARIATION

For a stronger-flavored cinnamon filling, use packed light or dark brown sugar in place of granulated sugar, and Vietnamese or Chinese cassia cinnamon.

Chocolate Glaze

Makes about ½ cup (125 mL)

Sometimes a pastry just calls out for a drizzle of chocolate. This easy method also results in easy cleanup.

INGREDIENTS

½ cup (125 mL) small semisweet chocolate chips

2 tbsp (25 mL) heavy or whipping (35%) cream

METHOD

1 In a small microwave-safe sealable plastic bag, combine chocolate chips and cream. Seal and microwave on High for 30 seconds. Remove the bag and knead the mixture until smooth and well blended.

2 Cut a tiny corner from the bottom of the bag and squeeze glaze over a cooled loaf in a decorative pattern.

TIP

If you use larger, button-size chocolate chips, it might be necessary to microwave on High for 15 to 30 seconds longer, until the chocolate has melted enough to knead smooth.

Cinnamon Sugar

Makes about $\frac{1}{4}$ cup (50 mL)

Like everything else, there is a difference between ready-made and homemade cinnamon sugar — and it's the degree of cinnamon-iness. I prefer to use the strongest type of cinnamon, that which is grown in Vietnam and labeled either Vietnamese or Saigon cinnamon. Use this mixture to make cinnamon rolls, to sprinkle on hot beignets or to make great cinnamon toast.

INGREDIENTS

$\frac{1}{4}$ cup (50 mL) granulated sugar

$1\frac{1}{2}$ tsp (7 mL) ground cinnamon

METHOD

1. In a small bowl, combine sugar and cinnamon until well blended.

Easy Artisan Glaze

Makes about 1¼ cups (300 mL)

Add a final sweet touch to your baked goods with a homemade glaze, thinner than either a frosting or an icing. A glaze is meant to give baked goods a sweet sheen and an initial flavor. Make glaze right before you're ready to use it; otherwise, it can harden and get lumpy.

INGREDIENTS

1 cup (250 mL) confectioner's (icing) sugar

¼ cup (50 mL) whole milk, half-and-half (10%) cream or heavy or whipping (35%) cream

1 tsp (5 mL) vanilla extract

METHOD

1 In a small bowl, whisk together confectioner's sugar and milk until smooth. Whisk in vanilla. Use right away.

Almond Glaze

Use 1 tsp (5 mL) almond extract in place of the vanilla.

Coffee Glaze

Use 1 tsp (5 mL) coffee extract in place of the vanilla, or substitute 2 tbsp (25 mL) freshly brewed strong coffee for half the milk.

Lemon Glaze

Use 1 tsp (5 mL) lemon extract or grated lemon zest in place of the vanilla.

Orange Glaze

Use ¼ cup (50 mL) freshly squeezed orange juice in place of the milk and 1 tsp (5 mL) orange extract or grated orange zest in place of the vanilla.

Cider Glaze

Use ¼ cup (50 mL) unsweetened apple cider in place of the milk.

Cider Glaze with Rum

Use ¼ cup (50 mL) unsweetened apple cider and 1 to 2 tbsp (15 to 25 mL) light or dark rum in place of the milk.

Cherry Glaze

Use ¼ cup (50 mL) cherry juice in place of the milk and 1 tsp (5 mL) almond extract in place of the vanilla.

Cranberry Orange Glaze

Use ¼ cup (50 mL) cranberry juice in place of the milk and 1 tsp (5 mL) orange extract or grated orange zest in place of the vanilla.

Mousseux

ACKNOWLEDGMENTS

Easy Bread might carry my name, but it's a team effort. My heartfelt thanks goes to publisher Bob Dees, editor Kathleen Fraser, photographer André Noël, food stylist Simon Roberge, and everyone at Robert Rose for making *Easy Bread* so delicious.

INDEX

A

B

C

D

E

F

G

H

I

L

R

S

T

Z

Library and Archives Canada Cataloguing in Publication
Title: Easy bread : 100 no-knead recipes / Judith Fertig.
Other titles: 100 no-knead recipes | One hundred no-knead recipes
Names: Fertig, Judith, author.
Description: Includes index.
Identifiers: Canadiana 20210148772 | ISBN 9780778806844 (softcover)
Subjects: LCSH: Bread. | LCSH: Baking. | LCGFT: Cookbooks.
Classification: LCC TX769 .F48 2021 | DDC 641.81/5—dc23